It's All About The Dash

Martin C. Nyman

FIRST EDITION

Cover design by Martin C. Nyman

Book design by Publishing Push

ISBNs
Paperback: 978-1-80227-700-5
eBook: 978-1-80227-701-2

CONTENTS

I dedicate this book to my family, my friends and my support network

PREFACE

This book takes its title from the Linda Ellis poem 'The Dash.' The dash is the little line that you see on grave-stones with a date of birth to the left of it and the date of death to the right of it. The dash is all about what you did between these dates. As an ex-serviceman and undertaker, I have experienced both highs and lows whilst wearing the Queen's Crown, and subsequently, in a second career within the funeral business. This book sets out to highlight some of the many funny, light-hearted and occasionally downright stupid things that happen in life, quite often unseen by the general pop-ulus. Above and beyond, this book also identifies one man's journey in the fight against the impact of effects on his mental health, plus the myriad of interventions required when attempting to regain mental well-being.

I spent thirty-five years serving in the Royal Navy and have had experiences that I wouldn't change, some good and some less so. Having kept diaries for many of these years and with old fashioned photographs to help, I intend to take you on a journey through my fifty-year working 'dash'.

My working 'dash' began at fifteen years of age and my intention is to focus more on the crazy things I've done with the occasional reference to operational duties. I hope you enjoy the black humour and are not offended by any of the content. Please enjoy.

CHAPTER 1
SHOOT NO SHOOT

Let me set the mood. I am serving onboard HMS Campbeltown, a capital ship in the Persian Gulf. We are between the first and the second gulf wars and tensions are very high. Due to our advanced equipment, we are dispatched on anti-aircraft picket duties to within eight miles of the Iraqi coast, just to the North-East of Kuwait City. Because the Iraqis are using mobile missile launchers for their Scud and Patriot missile systems, intelligence is struggling to tie down their positions. We are sent in each night under the cover of darkness with no obvious radar switched on and no weapon systems allowed to transmit. I am closed up in the operations room each evening along with my weapons teams but acting in a passive role. Lookouts are strategically placed on the upper deck as our first line of defence in case of a missile launch against us. Realistically, if a lookout saw a flash on the horizon and reacted quickly enough, we would still be hard pushed to respond in time because of the close proximity of the enemy and the effectiveness of modern missiles.

This tasking might be high risk but it's not suicidal. We had at our disposal a system called 'doppler radar'. Doppler radar works completely differently from conventional radar in that it doesn't transmit. With conventional systems, a pulse of radar energy is transmitted from the source until it finds something to rebound off. The pulse is then returned to the source unit giving the range, course and speed of the target. The downside of this system is that the enemy can look back down the transmitted pulse to see where it came from and in so doing it gives away our position. Doppler radar is passive and it 'listens' to the air. There is no pulse sent out from the ship. Doppler radar works in conjunction with our main air defence missiles and responds to air turbulence. We can pre-set parameters into the system effectively telling it to respond above a certain threshold. When doppler radar senses air turbulence exceeding pre-set parameters, it spawns numerous tracks on the weapons desk and alerts the operator to the possibility that something is there. Under normal circumstances, our missile system would be automatically linked to the doppler radar, and, unless we intervened, it would launch missiles in our defence. This entire system was designed to take away human error and reduce response times.

Rules of Engagement or ROE are very complex and rarely straightforward. They are designed to make sure that any act of force, particularly lethal force, is strictly legal and in keeping with pre-established criteria. To that end, Commanding Officers retain the right to veto any engagement at any stage. What this actually does is slows down our response capability. On one of these night patrols, we were closed up; it was about three in the morning and we were sat right in the middle of a no-fly zone. Nothing is allowed into our area as it then potentially becomes a legitimate target. As part of a coalition, all forces involved understand this. It was very quiet when all of a sudden, my doppler radar started to generate tracks on my system. My missile launchers swung around in response to being alerted but were being held on the 'safe to fire' switches awaiting Command approval. By now, the captain was standing behind me and looking into my monitor. He patted me on the shoulder and ordered "weapons free", which is my permission to release missiles. I waited, deliberating; something wasn't right. I then made my decision, and, after a few short seconds that seemed to last forever, I held fire. Remembering that I was at this point solely responsible for every life on board our ship, I decided against my captain's advice to release missiles. I had witnessed these circumstances in the simulator back at HMS Dryad when we had played war games. I was convinced that doppler radar was telling me that it was a helicopter and I knew our enemy had none in theatre. Almost immediately, radio silence was broken by an American helicopter who was flying straight through the no-fly zone and was en route to insert a SEAL team ashore. He had totally ignored all of the rules and had risked the lives of everyone on board that helicopter. The captain went ballistic at the pilot's stupidity and drafted a very strongly worded report. I was just grateful that I hadn't engaged the helicopter because given the range and his speed, it would have been a certain kill. The moments that led up to this action have haunted me all this time. What if I had got it wrong? A SEAL team and an aircrew all killed, plus a helicopter down; or worse, three-hundred dead sailors and a warship. Sometimes carrying out actions is easier than refraining from carrying out actions.

This was not my first experience of what is known as blue on blue or potential blue on blue engagements. During Desert Storm as the Americans called it, or Operation Granby as we knew it back in 1991, my then brother-in-law, Tam, was serving with the Queen's Own Highlanders. His regiment was on patrol in an armoured vehicle convoy when two A10 Thunderbolt American tank-busting aircraft opened fire on them without any reason and destroyed two Infantry Fighting Vehicles or IFVs. Nine British troops were killed and twelve were seriously injured. Thankfully, after nearly a day of waiting, we found out that Tam was not on the casualty list.

The author approaching Kuwait City

Now, it is all too easy to condemn blue-on-blue action but occasionally, we get things wrong ourselves and sometimes with potentially devastating implications. I was serving on board HMS Aurora during the late 1970s when the Northern Ireland troubles were at their peak. The Royal Navy had a small patrol vessel that was used to patrol Carlingford Lough on the border between the Republic of Ireland and Northern Ireland. This is a very short crossing between the two and an area favoured for smuggling firearms and explosives into Northern Ireland. The patrol craft needed essential repairs and a dock down period and so we were tasked with covering her duties. On one particular day, we observed a fairly large sailing boat behaving unusually, about six miles offshore. It was sitting very low in the water which raised our suspicions and then she refused to answer numerous attempts to call her on the radio. When radio failed, we flashed morse code at her using our large signalling lights, again to no avail. We then started to escalate our actions by manoeuvring across her intended course and would ordinarily have used our helicopter to investigate further, but it was tied up elsewhere, on other activities. After numerous attempts at contacting the sailing vessel and in keeping with our rules of engagement (ROE), the captain decided that we would fire a shot across the bow. This is where we shoot live ammunition ahead of the ship of interest. Again, after the single shot was fired, there was still no response. The single shot was followed by a burst from our 20mm Oerlikon, again ahead of the sailing vessel. At this point, she began to alter course towards us just as we were readying to fire into the vessel. As she altered course, we could see for the first time why she was sitting so low in the water; there were about forty or so schoolchildren on a day trip lining both sides of the boat. They had remained hidden from us by the belly of the mainsail in much the same way as we had remained unseen to them. They were totally oblivious to us being there. The skipper admitted that he had had the radio turned off. What could have happened doesn't bear thinking about. Incidentally, the following year, this area gained notoriety when twelve soldiers from the

Second Battalion Parachute Regiment lost their lives in an ambush at Warren Point.

I'd like to share one more 'operational story' with you at this point. If you believe in fate or luck, then this story would suggest that something was going right for us on this particular day. It was the twelfth of October 2000, and, whilst serving onboard HMS Cumberland, we had just finished our transit through Suez and into the Red Sea. We had some minor equipment defects and needed some fuel and so we were programmed to go into Aden Harbour in Yemen to rectify these two issues. Just before we started our approach, we were re-directed away from Yemen and on to Dubai to fuel and effect the repairs, and so we made our way through the Gulf of Oman to Dubai. Unbeknown to us, an American warship, USS Cole, had made her way into Aden in our place, as her needs were more urgent than ours. Shortly after berthing, the news broke that USS Cole had been attacked by two suicide bombers in a small boat that had been packed out with explosives. A massive twelve-by-eighteen-metre hole had been blasted in her port side killing seventeen American sailors and injuring thirty-seven. Immediately, all coalition ships were put to sea whilst the threat was reassessed. I was very grateful that we had been re-programmed and sent on to Dubai as the potential outcome could have involved us instead of the Cole.

CHAPTER 2
BASIC TRAINING

Imagine, if you can, quite some years earlier; this was where my 'working dash' began.

It was cold, it was dark and it was wet, and yet the long journey hadn't begun; neither literally nor figuratively. I was waiting with about a hundred or so other fifteen-year-old schoolboys at Holborn careers office in April of 1972 for our transport to leave. After a cramped journey that was far too long with only one toilet stop, we arrived at Shotley Gate near Ipswich in Suffolk. Our destination in East Anglia was HMS Ganges, the Royal Navy training establishment, where it was even colder, darker, and wetter. My life with the Royal Navy had begun.

We were taken to what is called the annexe, which is like a processing centre for Ganges and is set apart from the main establishment; this was to be our home for the next six weeks. On our arrival, we were given a mug of hot soup and a bread roll and shepherded into a hall for a briefing. Once briefed on the domestic set-up, we were shown to our accommodation and our respective beds. As it was fairly late by now, it was strongly suggested that we get as early a night's sleep as possible. The silence of the night was shattered by a horrible noise that would become the norm over the next nine months of basic training - the dreaded 'call the hands.' Call the hands is a pipe made on a bosun's call, which is a sort of funny-shaped whistle that has been used in the navy for centuries to communicate information. This wake-up call is passed over a tannoy system so it is very loud. I was now feeling both lonely and frightened with what I had taken on. I was used to Mum waking me up for school and, only three short months later, here I was in this strange and alien world.

The next few days were a whirlwind of activity with kit issues and haircuts (no scissors here), lectures and schooling, marching practise and rifle training and learning how to do basics like ironing and sewing, and cleaning of both ourselves and our kit! After about three or four days, we were marched over to the main establishment for our medicals. I have one slightly strange memory of our medicals and that is the doctor, who was a very portly female Army Officer who seemed obsessed with our balls. As we went through, we were each told to drop our shorts and underpants and she cupped our balls before telling us to cough. She then allowed us to move on through the medical which was very thorough. I say this was slightly strange because for the nine-month duration of our stay at Ganges, if you went to the sickbay for anything, she got you to drop your shorts and under-pants, cupped your balls, and instructed you to cough. One of our recruits got an ear infection and guess what? Check the balls; strange.

The first six weeks flashed by and although some had already left, most of us had made it this far. Today was the big move into the main establishment. After cleaning and packing up, we placed our suitcases and kit-bags on the transport and watched it disappear before we were marched across. On our arrival, there seemed to be a slight change in training tactics with everyone shouting and barking out orders. Our new divisional staff made themselves known and we were split into divisions. Everything was done at the double, which means double pace or running. Upon our arrival at our new 'home', we were given a full tour and shown our new duties.

I wish to digress a little. Much later in life, I was fortunate enough to visit San Francisco and took a trip to the island prison that is Alcatraz. The moment I set foot in the prison, it took me immediately back forty-five years to HMS Ganges. Cold dark stone walls smelling of damp, iron pipework running along the ceilings, solid concrete floors, bars on all windows and vents, com-pletely open and communal showers and a feeling of inescapability. Wow, the feeling was tangible!

Okay, back at Ganges, once you could adjust to the pace of training and the vast range of topics covered, you could begin to get into a routine. I'm not saying it was easy; it certainly wasn't, but achievable it was. I think my autistic tendencies may well have helped me. I think in black and white, no grey areas; finish something properly before I move on, everything has its place, etc., etc. One area that I particularly excelled in and enjoyed was mast-manning. Ganges has a mast that is one hundred and forty-two feet or forty-three metres tall. I'm not particularly good with heights so I took the mast as a challenge. Everyone was expected to climb the mast up to the first stage but beyond that point was optional. Only when the weather conditions were good were we allowed to go any higher. Over a period of three or four months, I mastered the mast until I could finally stand on the button at the top, stand up and salute. I considered this a massive achievement both personally, as I didn't have a good head for heights, and professionally, as it was much more than the staff expected of me.

I'd like to try to take you on a journey with me up the famous Ganges mast. With good weather conditions and little or no wind, we were allowed to climb this forty-three-metre monster that held so much fear for so many. The journey begins on the lower rigging which is like very heavy-duty netting, the squares being about six inches apart. Up we go clearing the safety net which is set at about eight feet or two point four metres above the ground. Every six feet or so, there was a vertical steel girder sticking upwards out from the ground which was part of the support for the safety netting. These girders put the fear of God into you because if you fell, it would be a lottery as to whether you fell on a girder and probably killed yourself or whether you would be fortunate enough to land on a section of safety netting. Okay back to the climb; we are passing through a height of about three double-decker buses as we approach the first yard-arm, and we are climbing upwards at about forty-five degrees to the ground. The first stage is at sixty feet or eighteen metres. As we approach the first stage, we have to negotiate one of the most frightening aspects of the ascent - the Devil's Elbow. We stop climbing forwards and upwards at about forty-five degrees and turn backwards on ourselves so that we are now climbing with the ground completely underneath our backs and we are hanging upside down. We are now climbing at about one hundred and thirty-five degrees to the ground. Over and around Devil's Elbow we go, steadying our nerves as we do so. The rigging that we are now climbing up is considerably smaller in its size and links up the first stage to the half-moon which is much further up. We climb through the second yard-arm at a height of eighty feet or twenty-four metres and climb very cautiously towards the half-moon and third yard-arm, at which point we are at a height equivalent to towering above Westminster Abbey. Once at the half-moon, there is room for only two people and no more conventional rigging to climb on. From now on, the climb focuses on a Jacob's ladder to ascend from the half-moon to the cow-horns. The cow-horns are two gaffs sticking out from the mast horizontally, each about ten inches wide and set considerably higher than a ten-storey block of flats at one hundred and eight feet or thirty-three metres. Now life becomes crazy. The last fifteen feet or four point six metres is climbed by shinning up the mast itself without aids. Now bear in mind that this is the early 1970s and modern-day trainers were yet to become readily available, so we are shinning up this fifteen-foot pole with a naval uniform on and plimsolls from the 1950s. These plimsolls are fine if everything is bone dry but as slippery and scary as hell if there is the slightest hint of moisture. On reaching the button, things change quite dramatically; using the two mainstays of the mast to assist you to get high enough to sit on the button, you become instantly aware of your height. This is because suddenly there is nothing above you, but an awful lot of distance below you. You sit for a few moments to catch your breath and to build up the courage for the last and most difficult part of the climb - standing up! With absolutely nothing above you and just a metal conductor sticking out from the button by about eighteen inches, you have to pull your feet up under your backside until you can shift your weight to your feet then very tentatively you start to straighten out. You have a deathlock on the conductor

The famous mast

until you are confident enough to stand tall, place the conductor between your knees and salute. You are now standing unaided up among the gods, feeling terrified and immensely proud in equal measures. What a start to a career.

One of the Ganges' sporting highlights was the boxing. My friend Andy Richards suggested that he and I should enter. I told him that I didn't know the first thing about boxing and that I would get slaughtered. He said that we could learn together as we went along. Andy then pointed out that there were rewards for entering, in the form of sweets. For just entering, you got three bars of chocolate, Mars, Crunchie, Twix, etcetera; if you won a fight, you got five bars. I should probably point out at this stage that whilst we were at Ganges, we were paid just twenty pounds a month, of which ten pounds was taken at source and paid into a Post Office Savings Account. These accounts were started when we joined and were compulsory. We were not allowed access to the account until we left Ganges. Payday fell every two weeks and you received your five pounds in a very formal naval manner. When your name was called, you answered "sir", stepped up to the pay officer and saluted. At the same time, you offered your open left hand and said your ship's book number, which was part of the official number that stays with you throughout your career. As you were receiving your pay, the Chief Gunnery Instructor stood to one side picking up people for haircuts. With your money in hand, the next stop was the NAAFI shop; it's like a small supermarket. Here you spent most of your fiver on cleaning gear like toothpaste, soap and shampoo plus boot polish and gym-shoe whitener. You would also buy a few stamps so that you could write home. Additionally, if you had been picked up, you went for a haircut, only this one you had to pay for. If anything was left, and it really wouldn't be very much, you could treat yourself to a bar of chocolate or two. Suddenly, and in context, boxing for sweets didn't seem so crazy.

Andy and I were the only two volunteers from our division and so we were drawn against one another. ABA rules, three, three-minute rounds, and so my boxing career began. As the bell rang, Andy and I stepped towards each other, me with a smile on my face and Andy looking very serious. Andy hit me square on the nose, which exploded, with blood going everywhere. It hurt, and my eyes were watering so much that I could hardly see. Realising that this was two boxers and not two friends in the ring, I protected myself as best I could until the bell rang. I knew there were two rounds left but I didn't relish getting hurt again so my whole demeanour changed. I became focused and much more aggressive. This time, I was giving as much, and more than I was receiving. After three rounds, I was awarded the fight and my five bars of chocolate, which made it all seem worthwhile. I found out afterwards that Andy hadn't been entirely honest with me as he had fought as a schoolboy and had eight fights under his belt. This made the win feel even better.

Towards our mid-term at Ganges, I was awarded class leader and wore a stripe on my uniform for which I was extremely proud. This was also when I first began to apply my style of leadership, although I wasn't as yet aware that I was doing it. I felt very strongly that if

15 years old & they gave me a gun

I wanted someone to do something for me then I had to be prepared to do it myself. I encouraged people to follow my lead by motivating them and not by barking orders at them. This style of leadership was to hold me in good stead for the remainder of my career and beyond.

As we moved towards the end of our time at Ganges, I was really hopeful that I would be able to be the button boy for our ceremonial leaving divisions, or parade. Training divisions happened every week as did ceremonial divisions. On our last training divisions before selecting who would provide both the guard and mast-manning crew, we were on parade and doing rifle training when a guy called Mike Smith, who was in the rank in front of me, made a costly mistake with his rifle drill. For those in the know, it was the movement from the order to the shoulder. For those not in the know, it is when the rifle is thrown from the ground up the right-hand side of the body and pulled in at the waist. Mike almost got it right but his bayonet almost completely severed his right earlobe. One of the staff stepped in and took him, bleeding, to the sickbay, and guess what…. yes, he had his balls checked. I never made button boy for our exit parade, which was a shame because my family had travelled up to see it and it would have been lovely, but I do have a dusty old photograph of my mastering the mast.

Nine months gone and to complete training, I was sent to HMS Cambridge on the outskirts of Plymouth for six further weeks. This was where gunnery training was taken to the next level. It also gave me my first taste of Plymouth, and particularly, the infamous Union Street. Although I didn't know it yet, this town would also become my home and the birthplace of my children in later life.

CHAPTER 3
MY FIRST SHIP

I joined HMS Hampshire in the spring of 1973 along with fifteen other young lads, all joining from HMS Cambridge. We were to make up the bulk of the gunnery division on this six-thousand-ton destroyer. Life after Ganges was so much more relaxed once on board. We were each given a part of the ship to work in and life proper began in the Royal Navy. After an initial settling period, something began to rear its ugly head again; this was something that I had seen in training but, as of yet, had not been part of - bullying! As we were the youngsters on board, we had to be in bed by ten-thirty until we had earned the right to be up late, or indeed, go ashore. Additionally, the Leading Hand of the mess had certain obligations to keep us safe and well as we were still under age. One of these duties involved protecting us from bullies. Now, for some reason, two members of the mess, one called 'Middy' Middleton and one called 'Ginge' Ackerman, had been picking me out from the crowd. Every night, when they came back from drinking ashore in Portsmouth, they chose to wake me up and threaten me with violence. They wouldn't let me sleep and did things like pulling my bed apart and throwing it on the floor. All the loneliness and negative feelings came back and I didn't know how to deal with the two of them. This was at a time when you didn't go complaining about these sorts of things; you were just expected to get on with life. Now, I am not a violent person, far from it, but with every occasion of bullying, I was becoming more and more riled inside. Compared to Middy, I was tiny - you could count my ribs just looking at me - whereas Middy, the main perpetrator, was very much larger, albeit mostly fat. One night, we had all turned in after a particularly busy day when I got my usual violent shake from Middy. Now, having been asleep, I wasn't in the mood for any of his shenanigans. Middy pulled the bedding off my bed and I felt something inside say enough is enough so I jumped out of my middle bunk and put my hand into the face of this drunken bully. The side gulch where we all lived was very restricted and tight so I pushed him backwards with my hand in his face until we were in the mess square which still had some lights on and lots more space. I hit him, just the once and not the best punch ever, but he fell onto the floor and surprisingly, he didn't try to fight back; probably too drunk. Whilst he was on the floor, I told him that that was enough of the bullying and that it was to stop. Unbeknown to me, Harry, the Leading Hand of the mess, had seen and heard the kafuffle from his gulch, so he came into the mess square and told Middy and Ginge to go to bed, which they did without question. Harry pulled me to one side and said that it was an offence to strike somebody in authority and that I shouldn't make a habit of it. He also said, with a smile on his face, that what he had seen was poetic justice and that there would be no further action. I never had a single repeat of bullying from either of these two thugs which, for me, made life so much more pleasant.

After a few months on board, the sixteen of us who had joined together earned the right to take leave in Portsmouth until midnight. This was a great feeling of freedom and we could at last sample the nightlife. A crowd of us found a bar called the 'Casbah'. They had a pool table, a dartboard, a jukebox and, most importantly, a landlord who would serve sixteen-year-olds. On one of these nights in our 'regular', I met a young lady and we hit it off straight away. We chatted and played pool and drank together. She told me that she had to be home by ten and asked if I would like to walk her home, which I did. When we got back to what was her parents' house, she introduced me to her mum and dad and made some coffee. Shortly after this, her parents retired for the evening which I thought was a little odd as it was relatively early. We started petting as soon as they were gone and things developed into full sex on the carpet. I say full sex, but this was me losing my virginity, so how full it was I don't really know. Suddenly, I was hit with this terrible stench! I almost gagged. I thought surely a woman can't smell this bad and I wondered whether it was normal or not. I wanted to ask but didn't think this would be such a good idea. As this was my first time, I had nothing to compare it to. By now, I had carpet burns on my knees as I had been pushing her across the room. Where we had ended up was next to one of these old-fashioned gentlemen's chairs, the ones with longer legs, and underneath the chair was a big pile of cat diarrhoea! I felt quite sick, but also relieved that there was an explanation.

Once our ship completed its refit and trials period, we were deployed to Cyprus as part of a peacekeeping force, as the Turks had just invaded Northern Cyprus. All combat had ceased but tensions were high so we had to stay about half a mile off Akrotiri at anchor. As ours was essentially a policing role, we were allowed ashore for sports and limited social activity. It was one of these sporting afternoons that led to something I would remember, in detail, for the rest of my life.

I was making my way to the boat embarkation jetty along with other members of the sports teams. We had about an hour until the boat was due so we went into the mess at RAF Akrotiri. A few of the less sport-minded chaps had decided to drink in their mess instead of playing sport. I got myself an orange juice at the bar and then noticed John Mendez in the corner looking totally distraught. John was one of the original sixteen gunners. When I asked John what was wrong, as he had obviously been crying, he said that he had rung home earlier from the mess and had been given some bad news. I never questioned what news as I could see he was totally distraught. John had spent all day drinking ridiculously cheap alcohol and was now completely in a bucket. The time to go approached and so we made our way to the boat embarkation point. I stayed with John trying to be supportive, but, at this point in my life, I had few or no life skills to fall back on. Never mind, he was a mate, and he needed help. We, along with everybody else, walked down towards the now-approaching boat when suddenly, John ran off into the darkness and towards the sea. In he went fully dressed and swimming away from shore as best he was able. I, still in sports gear, ran after him, stripping off what I could in the process. By now, he had disappeared into the darkness and as I entered the water, I shouted for someone to get the liberty boat to help us. I am quite a strong swimmer, thankyou Mum and Dad, and knew that as I had a lot less on than him, I should be able to reach him. After just a few short moments, I caught up with John and tried to reason with him but he wouldn't listen and swam out even further. Then, for some strange reason, my lifesaving training came to the front of my mind so when I caught up with John, I gave him a good ducking. Once he had swallowed a little water, he became much more receptive.

John was at the point of exhaustion and couldn't swim any more so I turned him onto his back, put his head next to mine, supported him under the chin and swam backwards until my feet could touch the stones beneath us. John was both distraught and exhausted so it really didn't help when the Petty Officer in charge of the boat had a go at him. The ten-minute journey by boat was punctuated by occasional digs by the Petty Officer about John's behaviour, which really wasn't helping as he had no idea what John was going through. We arrived at the ship and climbed a ten-foot ladder where we were met by the Duty Officer and the Quartermaster. Having collected our station cards - these are a way of the ship knowing who is onboard and who is ashore - we made our way up onto the flight deck.

At this point, the Duty Officer began where the Petty Officer had left off, berating John. Once more, John had had enough and he launched himself over the ship's side and into the ocean. I couldn't believe what I had been hearing and seeing but John was swimming off into the darkness again. I was not a great lover of heights but from about twenty feet up, I jumped in after him again. As I jumped, I screamed at the Quartermaster to get the lifebelt and ring ready to throw as I knew I was fairly exhausted and didn't know for how long I could swim. Thankfully, I caught John very quickly as he was stationary having taken in more water. By now, I was knackered and called out for the lifebelt which was thrown in our direction. I swam to it and then dragged it to John where I put my hand through the ring and placed it around John's neck. Too tired to swim, I called the Quartermaster to pull us in, which they did. John spent the night in sickbay under the watchful eye of the Doc. The next day, John was moved into RAF Akrotiri as the ship was sailing. John re-joined the ship later in the programme in Malta. I have felt a massive sense of pride every time I think back on this sequence of events. Furthermore, I know John is happily married with children and living in Carlisle.

Let us now lighten the mood. During one of our days whilst at anchor off Cyprus, the captain allowed the ship to go to 'Hands to Bathe'. This is essentially allowing us to swim from the ship. There are quite a few actions that need to be taken prior to allowing sailors to jump in the sea. Scrambling nets need to be rigged and lowered over the ship's side as do climbing ropes. A boat must be manned and in the water with a rifleman in it to act as shark watch. Machinery must be made safe like propellers and intakes and sonar and discharges. Once everything is in place, then a broadcast is made "Hands to Bathe". Everyone who can takes the opportunity to jump or dive in and cool off. Swimming in the open sea is not like swimming off the beach as you can only see a short distance due to the swell and waves and you have an enormous feeling of depth underneath you. Well, just about everyone that could be in the sea was, even the skipper. It was extremely hot and the swim was very welcome. After twenty minutes or so, one or two of the guys on board were gesturing towards the sea and seemed concerned. The sea boat headed off at speed toward whatever the concern was and slowly everybody was latching on to the fact that something wasn't quite right. People began climbing out of the ocean using the scrambling nets and the ropes, and, although there was no panic, something seemed wrong. I looked towards where the sea boat was and could just catch a glimpse of the rifleman pointing his gun down into the sea.

This was enough for me, so I swam to the nets and climbed the fifteen feet or so on board. Once on board, I could see what the concern was; there were sharks and lots of them. The bridge sounded the main broadcast alarms and told everyone to leave the water quickly and calmly. The sharks were swimming ever closer and by now, almost everyone was clear of the water, everyone except our intrepid Physical Training Instructor known as Clubz. Clubz was on his back and just relaxing and oblivious to anything that was going on. He was about ten metres or so from the ship when he opened his eyes and looked up at about two hundred sailors looking down at him and pointing. He looked to his right and saw the fins of the first of the sharks and they were huge. Clubz managed to swim to the ship and scale a rope in what must have been a world record; if you had blinked you would have missed it. One thing that didn't sit right at this point is why the boat's crew, and particularly the rifleman, had not engaged the sharks. The answer was simple these were large basking sharks migrating and they are harmless to humans. The coxswain of the boat had confirmed this on the radio with the captain, who was by now on board, and they had agreed not to shoot at the sharks.

Whilst we are on the subject of sharks, I would like to share another story with you that happened a year later whilst in the Caribbean. Occasionally, in naval life, a golden opportunity to do something completely different presents itself. Our Navigating Officer, a really nice chap called Bill who was an avid sailor, was also a qualified Offshore Skipper with the Royal Yachting Association or RYA. The Armed Forces had a yacht called 'Adventurer' which had just competed and been very successful in the 'Whitbread Round the World Race'. The race now over, they were looking for volunteer crews to sail the boat back to the UK in different legs. Bill had managed to negotiate a fantastic twelve-day leg in the Caribbean culminating in a stop in Puerto Rico. Six volunteers were needed and I was fortunate enough to be one of them.

We raced the boat at night which is no mean task and stopped at some beautiful islands during the days. Having picked the boat up in Trinidad and Tobago, we moved through islands such as Martinique, St. Vincent, St. Lucia and the Virgin Isles. Our idyllic daily routine comprised of anchoring or berthing just after sunrise, a swim before breakfast on board and then ashore for a look around, hopefully finding a beach spot for lunch and a glass of wine (it's what the yachties do). After more serious sunbathing at the beach, it was back on board for sun-downers (drinks) before we would wind things down ready to sail to the next island. This was about as good as life could get, and, as a side issue, we were also being taught to become qualified yacht hands with the RYA. It was with heavy hearts that we arrived at our last destination before re-joining our ship. Tonight was the first night that we hadn't been programmed to go to sea so Bill decided we would have a bit of a do and invite

Virgin Gorda & St. Lucia provide two of the most beautiful beaches you could wish for.

those local yachties on board for drinks. All preps went ahead, like cleaning and polishing, and getting everything ready for a party. As the sun set, one of the crew pointed out that we had very little Coke left and the two most popular drinks amongst the yachties are rum and Coke or gin and tonic.

We were berthed at a three-sided jetty and on the outermost berth. You could clearly see the Chandlers in the distance even though the light was fading fast. Bill asked if I would go and get a case of Coke from the Chandlers and handed me a twenty-dollar note. I decided that as we were all in swimming gear, the easiest thing to do would be to swim directly towards the Chandlers which had a light on it, and then walk back with the Coke along the three jetties. At this point, I dived in and started swimming.

By now, it was dark but my beacon was the light at the Chandlers. As I began my swim, which I suppose was about half a mile, two things unsettlingly entered my mind. Firstly, where we were, just off Puerto Rico, was the worst place in the world for fatal shark attacks, and secondly, the movie of the year, which had us all terrified, was Jaws. What were the chances?

My swimming became more urgent and I increased my stroke as the last of the light faded. I was focused on the Chandlery light in front of me when all of a sudden, my worst fears were realised. Something very large and very strong brushed my chest and then my stomach; whatever it was, it was very rough and abrasive to the touch. I was going into panic mode when I realised I had actually swum up the Chandlers' boat ramp and had effectively beached myself on solid concrete. I think someone was watching over me that day.

Having now re-joined our ship, we resumed our deployment up the East Coast of the USA. When a warship visits a port of call, quite a bit of PR is carried out before her arrival in order to raise the profile of the visit. This publicity draws attention from local businesses, among others, that might wish to attract our sailors to spend money in their establishments. These might be swimming pools, sports centres, bars, restaurants, cinemas, bowling alleys, concerts, theatrical productions,

shops, and so the list goes on. Complimentary or con-
cessionary tickets are quite often left at the gangway so
that when the sailors go ashore, they can grab anything
that might be of interest to them. On one particular
night, I was going ashore with a crowd of my friends
and the Quartermaster suggested we take one of these
complimentary tickets to a local show. I grabbed a ticket
and put it in my back pocket without really looking at it.

We made our way into downtown Georgia and
found the local bars and clubs. One of these bars was
an Irish bar. Here, they served good beer at a good price;
they also sold good food. The barmaids were all dressed
to kill. There was a pool table and a dartboard. There
were redneck women who were just looking to have a
good time, and a well-stocked jukebox, with live music
to come later on. Needless to say, our first bar for a drink
was the last place we visited as we had everything we
needed. We stayed until very late and then made our
way back to the ship. It was only when I was putting my
laundry together the next morning that I took a look at
the ticket in my back pocket. It was a complimentary VIP
ticket including backstage passes to see Elvis Presley.
We had fifty of these complimentary tickets and only
five people went. My brother Booger is a massive fan
of Elvis and when I told him, he went bonkers calling
me all sorts. When I look back, I realise what a massive
opportunity missed it was, particularly, because he died
two years later.

One or two other short stories from this stage of my career include 'Jack the axe'. Jack was one of our fellow gunners and a little unorthodox in most things he did. He was about six foot five inches tall with a huge black beard. Jack always wore black clothing with heavy biker boots when not in uniform, and he attached his wallet to himself with a very heavy-duty chain. Jack's big thing was that he didn't like being touched. Unbeknown to anyone, Jack slept with a fireman's axe under his pillow. One particular night, someone had jokingly put Jack down for a wake-up call that he hadn't asked for. The Quartermaster (QM), knew of Jack's reputation but his Bosun's Mate (BM) was new and a little wet behind the ears. The BM took the shakes book and went about his duties of waking up everyone that had asked for a shake. When he tried to shake Jack, he was told where to go. As is his duty, he wouldn't leave unless he had a signature to say that he had shaken him. Without any warning, Jack produced this axe from under his pillow and launched it at the BM. The axe hit the pipework around Jack's gulch and wedged itself into the lagging. The BM left in a rush and the nickname 'Jack the axe' was born.

During some downtime in Portsmouth, I was invited to a party in Gosport. The party was for one of the WRNS' birthdays and about a dozen or so went across on the ferry for her party. Her flat was a small upstairs flat with ground floor access and she had set up things really nicely. The night turned ugly quite early when a gang of about fifteen or so bikers decided to hang about outside her flat drinking and letting her know that they intended to gatecrash the party. Needless to say, she was upset and didn't know what to do. What happened next impressed me so much that I remember all the details.

One of our party was a Physical Training Instructor (PTI) called Jock Doig. Now, Jock was a big fellow and very fit. He also came from the Gorbals in Glasgow which has its own no-nonsense reputation. It wasn't what Jock did next but how he did it that impressed me. Having removed his jacket, he went down the narrow stairway and proceeded to kick one of the bikes over causing a domino effect. About four or five bikes fell over causing an instant reaction from the bikers who headed straight for Jock. Jock very cleverly backed himself into the hallway which only allowed one person at a time to get in. How simple but how brilliant; only one could get at him at a time which he was more than capable of dealing with. With bloodied noses and a bruised reputation, the bike gang collected their bikes and left. Jock came back upstairs, put his jacket on and carried on drinking as if nothing had happened. When the police arrived expecting carnage, there was none, not even any evidence of a fight. They left more than happy with the outcome.

CHAPTER 4
THE MUCH TRAVELLED SAILOR

I joined HMS Dido, my third ship, in the spring of 1980, when she had just returned from operational deployment. Within a week or so of joining, the First Lieutenant, who is the second in command, started looking for volunteers to go to Hong Kong to work as part of the Illegal Immigration Operations. I didn't volunteer too quickly for two reasons; firstly, you are taught early in your career never to volunteer for anything as there will always be a catch, and secondly, as I had just completed my shore time, I felt that the other chaps should have the first shout as they had been operationally very busy. To my very pleasant surprise, not a single person volunteered so I put my hand up. What was to follow was probably the best six months of my entire career.

I flew out from RAF Brize Norton in Oxfordshire with numerous as yet unknown people, and, after a sixteen-hour flight, we arrived at RAF Kai Tak in Hong Kong. We were taken to the newly built tower block that was HMS Tamar and shown our accommodation. Four of us to a mess right on the edge of town - this was going to be quite some party.

Hong Kong is a phenomenal place to visit with so much to see and do but I am going to try to concentrate on the job that we were sent there to do. The pattern was simple; four days on patrol followed by four days off. On day two, we were taken to the boat that would be home for half of our stay; Her Majesty's Tug 'Clare'. Once on board, we met the skipper, an absolute gentleman called Charles Addis. He was a Lieutenant Commander, and his number two, an Australian Lieutenant called Jim, was also the navigator. There were two Hong Kong staff, Eddie the chef and Ben the translator. Apart from myself who was drafted in as the Buffer, responsible for seamanship, there was Buck the electrician, Tigger the engineer and Derek the communicator. Our duties were relatively straightforward; we would act as mother ship to the Royal Marine rigid raiders that were actively pursuing both illegal immigrants (ii's) and aiders and abetters (aa's). We would operate predominantly at night going on patrol just before sunset and finishing a patrol just after sunrise.

Acting as mother ship, we had the communications to direct and re-direct rigid raiders as necessary and when any ii's were caught, they would be brought to us for processing. This processing involved getting them onboard with Ben explaining what was happening all along, searching them, separating men from women, and then feeding them with rice and warm water. Once processed, the men were put in the hold area and the women remained on deck. Once we became full, we would call in the Hong Kong Police boat to take the ii's from us to a secure area ashore before being repatriated to China. The Hong Kong Police were quite vocal with the ii's and occasionally heavy-handed. Charles, the skipper, explained that many of the police officers themselves had started off as ii's leaving China for a better life and they felt that too many ii's might affect their livelihood. Staying with the skipper for a moment, Charles had written half a dozen books on the plight of the ii's and the ruthlessness of the aa's and was very learned in this area. One thing he taught us from day one was that if, when searching someone, we found any People's Liberation Army insignia, we were to ditch it straight over the side. This was because any PLA deserters were executed on their return to China and Charles would not be part of this.

Since we were the only boat with radar, we would quite often intercept boats ourselves, leaving the swimmers for the Royal Marines. Once any boat or craft was cleared, we had to sink it, which leads me to one amusing story and one serious story. Buck, our electrician, climbed into a boat that we had just cleared and we went about sinking it. He took his trusty hatchet and hacked away at the hull of the boat, when suddenly, the hatchet went through the hull and water came cascading in. Poor old Buck had got his hatchet stuck under the boat, and, with his hand through the safety strop, he couldn't leave the boat that was sinking beneath his feet. With water at knee level, Buck managed to free his hatchet and he climbed on board to his great relief and our great amusement.

The other story demonstrates the futility of the situation the ii's find themselves in. We were patrolling one night when we picked up a sizeable boat on radar. We made our way to the location of the boat and saw nothing untoward; however, we moved very close to the boat and saw that the bottom of it was lined with plastic coats and mackintoshes. It was only when we prodded the bottom of the boat with a boathook that we discovered about thirty ii's hiding under the coats. This behaviour seemed very strange to those of us who were seeing it for the first time, but the skipper had seen it before. The ii's don't understand radar; they think if they can't be physically seen, they'll get away. They also believe that the raincoats will hide them from radar. Whenever this happens, Charles gets a group of the ii's onto the bridge to try to educate them on how we are able to see them even in the dark. He does this in the hope that they will know not to try again.

One of the less savoury stories that came out of my time in Hong Kong involves a Royal Marine rigid raider and an ii. It was towards the end of a patrol when one of the rigid raiders saw an ii-swimmer making his way towards a Hong Kong beach. The raider gave chase but it was very late and the swimmer began making his way on foot out of the deeper water. Not to be outwitted, the Royal Marine made a bad error of judgement and pursued the swimmer up the beach at speed, unpinning his outboard in the process. This allowed the boat to travel through about eight inches of water. His boat launched into the air and hit the back of the swimmer's head, partially decapitating him in the process. Needless to say, this was not a satisfactory action and the Marine was arrested and charged.

HMT Clare

More Illegal Immigrants (ii's)

The author searching and safeguarding ii's

These young people are between 14 & 17 years of age. They will almost always have a contact address sewn into their swimming shorts. These addresses are important to the police in their efforts to reduce people-smuggling.

Whilst the ii's draw a lot of compassion, given the pathetic position they find themselves in, there is little or no compassion for the aiders and abetters (aa's). These are money-grabbing people who pay scant regard to life and thrive on the ignorance of the ii's. It is the aa's who organise fast boat trips from China to Hong Kong. They pack far too many ii's into the hull of the big powerboats, and these powerboats run much faster than anything the British forces have at their disposal. The powerboats race across at speeds in excess of sixty knots, throw everyone out, literally, then speed back into the sanctuary of Chinese waters. There had been two previous occasions where an aa had been tracked and so they slide into the water unseen by everyone and allow the powerboat to go on without a coxswain. Ultimately, the boat crashes, killing or injuring ii's whilst the aa escapes unseen. The only upside to this story is that the Hong Kong police impound these big powerboats and invite the owner to come and collect his property, which, of course, never happens. After six months, if the boat isn't collected, it gets a lovely coat of grey paint and a blue flashing light and wears an ensign. Now, we can compete with them for speed. When I left Hong Kong, there were six of these very fast 'patrol' boats.

Moving on from Hong Kong, I'd like to start this next part of my travels in the southern hemisphere, and, more specifically, my journeys to the southern oceans. Most organisations, businesses or clubs have some sort of initiation or qualification that falls somewhere outside of the norm. The Royal Navy is no exception and when crossing the equator, or crossing the line, as we call it, we follow age-old traditions in initiating our 'new blood'.

Preparations begin for crossing the line months earlier when certain key players need to forward-plan and organise certain items of stores that wouldn't ordinarily be carried. The ship's Chief Shipwright, or 'chippy' as we call him, contacts the sail-makers in the dockyard and commissions two canvas dunking pools which are about ten feet by ten feet and about three feet high. No money ever changes hands but the international currency of tea, coffee, sugar and biscuits secures its purchase. The ship's entertainment officer, yes there really is one, visits the printers in Barracks, and, carrying the same currency, he commissions enough 'crossing the line' certificates to accommodate the entire ship's company. Timber and cordage and spare bunting are also taken on board to be stowed away until needed. Sailors secrete all manner of unusual clothing and props in their secret stowages for use at the ceremony.

Okay, back on board and about two hundred miles north of the equator, things begin in earnest. On the eve of our arrival at 0 degrees latitude, a broadcast is made from the bridge to state that we are approaching King Neptune's Royal Domains. That evening, just after sunset, the quarter-deck hatch opens and out of the darkness step mysterious figures. The first to step out is one of Neptune's messengers with two 'bears' as escort. This is followed by a second and subsequently third team, each a repeat of the previous. These teams are welcomed on board by the captain and they make their way to the various mess decks on board. On arrival at the mess, they must be invited in and made to feel welcome, i.e., given a drink from the bar. The messenger then reads out a proclamation and lists those who are to be initiated the next day. If hospitality is less than expected, then members of that mess will be in for a difficult initiation the following day. Initiation is primarily for first-time crossers of the line; however, others may be added to the list so it is a good idea to behave yourself.

Overnight, the chippy and his team work into the wee small hours preparing everything on the flight deck, which is by now out of bounds to everyone else. The only major thing to do is fill the two pools with water, but because of the weight and the effect on stability, this is done after the last course change on the morning of crossing. Frantic, nervous and excited energy is being burned off below decks as everyone looks forward to what is coming next. And so, on a cue from King Neptune himself, (the chief stoker) and his beautiful queen (Wallie the gunner) the captain makes a broadcast to state that we are at the equator and all personnel are to muster on the flight deck.

King Neptune's messengers and bears

Police and bears in action

King Neptune and his Queen

Demon barber and doctor

Who's next?

The two thrones overlook the two dunking pools and there is a dunking stool for those to be initiated. Numerous strangely dressed policemen see that order is kept and the bears await their prey in the pools. Either side of the dunking stool is the barber and the doctor, again in very strange garb. The senior messenger then announces the first victim…. I mean, person, to be initiated and it is the youngest lad on board; poor thing, he looked petrified. So, having been seated on the dunking stool with his back to the pools, the ceremony begins. First up, the 'doctor', who emptied a large syringe (without needle) into his mouth. The contents of the syringe vary from ship to ship with the only rule being it must be edible. Our chef chose a wonderful cocktail of tuna fish, broccoli, raw eggs, milk, pepper, and tabasco sauce. Doing his best not to gag, which is totally forbidden until after the induction, young Jammie is lathered by the 'barber' for his shave. The lather is a mix of flour and water and all utensils are wooden so no unnecessary accidents. At this point, King Neptune allows the bears to take over and they tip the stool back and fully immerse Jammie and give him a damn good dunking before they throw him over into the next pool, where two more bears take over and dunk him again. Once this is done, he is thrown out of the pool and onto a gym mat where he can now recover. Music is playing, a beer stand is selling beer and a free barbeque is on the go so recovery doesn't take long. Then we start working through all of those uninitiated members of the ship's company, including two who tried to slip through the net, the Chief Bosun's Mate who, in twenty-five years of service, had never crossed the line, and none other than the captain who had tried very hard to keep it to himself.

Needless to say, fun was had by all and only two threw up which, given what was being put in their mouths, wasn't bad at all. That evening, certificates were handed out to everyone to say that they had crossed the line in keeping with King Neptune's criteria. Now, as an ancient mariner myself, these certificates are not to be sniffed at as they offer certain comforts. Admission to the realm of Seven Seas and Six Oceans allows us to fall overboard without sharks, dolphins, whales and eels either eating us, playing with us, or otherwise maltreating us. It also goes on to state that all Sailors, Soldiers, Marines and Globetrotters who have not crossed our royal domains must treat us with the respect that is due to one who has visited Neptune's domain.

Whilst serving on H.M.S. Aurora as a young seaman, I was fortunate enough to visit Rio De Janeiro in Brazil, just south of the equator. Having now fully recovered from our crossing the line ceremony, we were enjoying the benefits of being in a wonderful part of the world. What a beautiful place, and so full of life. Copacabana Beach was fantastic and Sugar Loaf Mountain with Christo Rei were spectacular. Well, the story that I wish to share with you only just gets me out of the dockyard in Rio. The first day ashore follows a fairly well-established pattern - that is, go ashore and buy your postcards and any souvenirs before you sample the bar life and clubs. Walking out from what is a very large dock area, suddenly, the relative tranquillity of the docks is overpowered by the hustle and bustle of downtown Rio.

Immediately outside the dockyard gate, I was drawn to a chap selling souvenirs, but not ordinary souvenirs; he was selling very large spiders and they were alive. Once the chap explained what happens, I watched him sell one to a tourist. Initially, from a large glass tank of about sixty spiders, you select which one you want. The seller then picks it out and places it in a clear liquid which kills and preserves it almost instantly; no Health and Safety standards here. He then places the now-dead spider on a white hardboard base and glues the base of the thorax and each of its legs to the board. He then places a dome-shaped plastic cover over the spider before placing a pre-made frame on top. After flipping the now-mounted spider, he secures everything with tacks. You now have a spider that was alive five minutes ago, framed and ready for travel. My youngest brother is a massive fan of big spiders and so I had to have one. The spiders I found out are 'Goliath Tarantulas' and are about the size of your hand. I picked my spider, he pickled it, we exchanged some money and I left with what I thought was a great souvenir for my brother.

That really should be the end of the spider story but it isn't. My brother loved it and placed it up out of reach on a shelf in his bedroom. There it sat for years, almost forgotten about. One day when I was home, the family were watching some TV while Mum was upstairs cleaning and doing her domestic chores. Suddenly, we heard an almighty scream and Mum came flying down the stairs. Once we could calm her enough to tell us what was wrong, she told us that there was a huge spider on my brother's bed and she was terrified. My brother and I went upstairs to find this massive spider only to find that his spider from Rio had been knocked off the shelf when she was dusting and, unbeknown to her, she had dislodged it. Unfortunately for Mum, it fell the right way up and onto a white sheet. Mum had only seen the spider in her peripheral vision and she was convinced it was alive. My brother found a new home for his spider where Mum didn't have to worry about it.

Another short story coming out of Rio De Janeiro involves the Great Train Robber, Ronnie Biggs. Ronnie Biggs was a robber who had been jailed after the 1963 Great Train Robbery and had escaped prison in 1965. He had been a fugitive for what would eventually be thirty-six years and after almost getting caught in Australia, made his way to Brazil and specifically Rio De Janeiro. Here, he got his girlfriend pregnant and married her which meant that he couldn't be extradited back to the UK. Well, whilst I was having my spider souvenir made up, the stockers' mess from H.M.S. Danae, which was berthed immediately astern of us, were ashore in town and met up with Ronnie Biggs by chance. After a few drinks, he was invited back on board. It is normal for sailors abroad to invite guests back for drinks and maybe something to eat. Astonishingly, Biggs agreed and went onboard Danae for drinks and a cheeseboard. After some time, the duty officer, an in-experienced midshipman, found out that Ronnie Biggs was in the stokers' mess, so he instructed the Leading Hand of the mess to escort Mr Biggs off the ship immediately, which he duly did. I remember watching him leave and they were saying goodbye as if they were all old friends. When the visit of Ronnie Biggs became known about, the Midshipman had his horoscope read by the captain who wasn't impressed that we had let go a fugitive who had voluntarily come onto sovereign soil (the warship). An opportunity missed to re-capture him. Ironically, in 2001, he gave himself up and flew by private jet, chartered by the Sun newspaper, back to the UK.

My time on Aurora didn't end too well as whilst we were serving in the Mediterranean, we visited what was then Yugoslavia, more specifically Split. Having by now been boxing for about six months, I was extremely fit and didn't think twice when I was asked to partake in an eight-mile mountain run with the resident American troops. After the 'fun run', as it was known, we were invited back to their mess for food and drinks. Now when I say drinks, I mean Raki. For those that don't know, Raki is a twice-distilled liquor with an anise flavour, and it is very popular in Turkey and the Balkans. It should also be drunk with water and certainly not by the bottle, which, of course, we ignored.

I was due to be playing volleyball for the ship the next morning, so, I got up in good time with a stinking hangover and began dressing for sports. This is when my world was turned upside down. I collapsed in the mess and had a fit, followed by a total seizure which is known as a grand mal. My heart stopped and my breathing stopped, and, if not for the PTI who was there, I would probably have died. I say this because apart from the Doc, the only other person trained in first aid is the PTI. He carried out cardiac massage and mouth-to-mouth resuscitation to bring me back. Once revived, our Doc got involved and organised a medical escort from the UK to come out to meet us in Italy, as we were sailing the next day. Once back in the UK, I was taken to Royal Naval Hospital Haslar for extensive tests and to recover. I hadn't realised the seriousness of my situation until the doctor explained exactly what had happened. I was offered to be released from the service and told in no uncertain terms that if it happened again, I would have no say in the matter.

Once released from hospital, I was sent home to properly recover. Whilst I felt fine in myself, my parents have said that from that day onwards, my character changed quite dramatically. Over the years, I have pressed them to elaborate on what they meant by 'character change'. According to my mum and dad, before the grand mal, I was laid back and easy-going with a fairly relaxed mindset. After the grand mal, and ever since, I have been more aggressive, more easily aggravated, shorter-tempered, much more easily stressed, with a shorter attention span, and so the list goes on. Changes or not, I survived and am forever in our PTI's debt. Incidentally, I have never touched Raki since.

Racism is not a subject that has raised its ugly head during my fifty-year 'working dash' very much, with two very notable exceptions. During the mid-1980s, whilst serving on board HMS Arrow, we were berthed in 'Bayside', Miami, and a crowd of us had gone ashore for a walk one hot and sunny afternoon. I think there were six of us who found this bar in downtown Miami, and, not understanding local politics, we went in for a drink. We were in a fairly run-down part of town, and a bit off the beaten track, but this was a very modern bar with a pool table and a decent jukebox. The bar itself was in the middle of the room and was circular, and the entrance was all one-way glass to help with heat distribution. With good air conditioning and a well-stocked bar, why not drink here?

The barman, who was black, seemed friendly enough and served us our drinks. The only other person in the bar was another black man who was sitting in the corner. He was extremely well-dressed and dapper with his long coat and hat. I should point out that our party consisted of five white guys and one black guy, Andy. Andy was one of our ship's company and the colour of his skin had never even been discussed before, let alone been an issue. The barman hinted about us being there, but he didn't make it clear enough that we shouldn't be drinking there. After about ten minutes, the big chap in the corner got up to leave; he headed towards the door and waited. Bear in mind that the entire wall was glass, so we were able to see an older white chap shuffling along the footpath; he was very unsteady on his feet. As the older white chap got in line with the door, the black guy pushed the door open quite violently. The door hit the white guy, knocking him over quite deliberately in the process. We stopped what we were doing and looked on in astonishment. The white chap was on the floor and moaning away to himself. The black guy stepped forward and over him in a very menacing fashion and said something like, "Do you want to make anything of it"? Needless to say, the white man said nothing, waited until the black man left, and then got up and shuffled off. This was our cue to leave, so we drank up and left. When we got back towards Bayside, we were told by another barman that we were very lucky not to have had any serious issues, particularly as we had both black and white in our group.

My second unexpected introduction to the world of racism came some fifteen years later in Durban, South Africa. During an earlier cocktail party, my friend James and myself had latched onto the local fire chief, a gentleman called Mike. Mike had a wicked sense of humour and we all got on really well. Mike invited James and me to come for dinner at his house and to meet his family. Mike picked us up in his pick-up truck and drove us to the outskirts of Durban, where he lived. It was dark as we arrived and pulled onto the drive at Mike's house. Mike pressed a remote button and the large steel gate began to slide open; the truck rolled in and Mike told us to stay in the car until he called us. He got out and disappeared from view for a moment or so. Mike then called us to him one at a time; this is when we realised that he had two large dogs sitting one on either side of him. These were obviously working dogs as there was no tail-wagging or excitement - just two dogs very focused on what was in front of them - us! We were told not to pet them nor speak to them so we of course complied. Mike led us into his home and we met his lovely family.

As much out of curiosity as anything else, I asked Mike about the security situation, having just witnessed the dogs and the gate routine. Mike said that since the recently abolished apartheid policies and the appointment of Durban's first black mayor, there had been a lot of racist crime. Murders were at an all-time high and certain areas of the city were now black-only. I asked the question, "So, what about the postman, the milkman or someone coming onto the property with a delivery?" Mike said that everyone knew that you don't go into someone's property; it's dangerous. Labouring the point, I said, "What about maybe a tourist that is lost and wants directions?" Mike said quite bluntly that the dogs would kill them! He went on to say that he had learned a little trick from the police chief, who was a friend of his; if someone is killed on your property, you have a legal responsibility to deal with them, but if you throw them over the fence onto the footpath, you have no legal obligation at all! That comment quite shocked me.

Because I had shown interest in the security side of things, Mike sent his twelve-year-old son to his room to get his 'gun'! The lad came back with what looked like a 9mm Beretta, which is a magazine-fed pistol. He handed me the gun and not only was it loaded (there was a magazine on the pistol), but it was also made ready (meaning a bullet was in the chamber). The only thing needed to fire this pistol was to remove the safety catch and squeeze the trigger. Twelve years old with this at his disposal - frightening! Mike then sent his eight-year-old daughter to her room where she retrieved a small 'Saturday night special' gun. Both James and myself had daughters around about her age and we both found this very hard to take in. Her gun was loaded and readied but she didn't really know how to use it properly yet. Mike said to his daughter, "What's that for, darling?"

She said, "If anyone comes into my room that I don't know, I point this at them and squeeze the trigger until it stops!" Wow, what a crazy world we live in.

Whilst we were in Durban, we also had the pleasure of meeting the local ex-servicemen's association. As we will discuss in later chapters, these are all old-timers who have done their bit for their country and are now happily retired. The opportunity arose for a trip out to 'Ladysmith'. Ladysmith is steeped in naval history. It is where HMS Powerful provided heavy guns in the battle against the Boers, and it is also where the modern-day field gun derives from. Whilst we were en route to Ladysmith, we went through a few townships that were very busy, bordering on chaotic. We stopped in traffic one time and a guy came over to clean the windscreen. The driver indicated no, but the man tried pushing his wares, so the driver produced a gun from the glove box and showed it to the gentleman. With a grunt and a moan, the window cleaner left us alone. Once we moved off, I asked the driver about what had just happened. Apparently, there had been a high occurrence of hijackings and the driver said he would have given him one more warning and then he would have shot him! I sat in silence for quite some time. I was struggling to understand how such hatred and scant regard for life could be so rife. My time in South Africa showed me that although Apartheid policies had been banned, there was still many years' worth of hatred between black and white communities.

CHAPTER 5
THE SINKING OF THE
YELLOWSTONE

My next story is a more serious account of something that happened back in 1978 in Cape Trafalgar, off Gibraltar. We had just sailed from Gibraltar and were carrying Flag Officer Gibraltar to an offshore position where he could review the submarine fleet that was available to him. On our way out to sea, a thick fog fell after what had been a beautiful day. With visibility down to about three hundred metres, we approached our rendezvous position pretty well on time. Four submarines were on the surface and were in line astern of one another and awaiting the Admiral's salute and steam-past. We passed at slow speed along the line of submarines with the captain of each saluting the Admiral from his respective tower. After social niceties had been exchanged, we went around and picked up speed for a steam-past, which was executed with military precision. As the afternoon went on, visibility reduced dramatically to maybe as little as

Submarine steam-past

twenty metres. Having now carried out our tasking, we turned to head back towards Gibraltar to return the Admiral. It was about then that we received an S.O.S. from two ships that had collided in thick fog further out in the cape. The Algerian registered IBN Batouta had struck and become entangled with the American-registered SS Yellowstone. As is the case in any S.O.S., any unit that is able to assist does so. The Admiral had a very important dinner party that evening so we decided to scramble our helicopter to fly him in, whilst we made best speed to the collision position. Our information at this point was that there were five dead and two serious injuries on board the American grain carrier but no

casualties aboard the Algerian freighter. H.M.S. Aurora
arrived at the scene early the next morning and the fog
had partially lifted. It was quite surreal seeing two very
large ships effectively welded together. The Batouta, a
modern freighter, had her bow wedged into the stern
and cabin quarters of the much older Yellowstone. As
I was the on-watch coxswain, I readied the ship's lifeboat,
as was my instruction, and the First Lieutenant, myself
and my two-man crew were lowered into the water to go
and evaluate the situation. Our arrival at the scene was
very sobering as there was an awful amount of crushed
and twisted metal. The survivors of the Yellowstone
were mostly in shock and didn't say much. We went
to the collision point which was inside the crew's cabin

I.B.N. Batouta meets S.S. Yellowstone

quarters. There, the reason for their shock was apparent; everything was crushed, blood and body parts were evident, and nothing was intact. The Batouta had struck the Yellowstone just above the waterline with her bulbous bow causing huge damage. The first priority was to get the dead and injured over to the Gibraltar guard ship now that she was in attendance, so, using her helicopter, that is indeed what we did. The next big issue was how to separate the two ships.

The ocean-going tug, which had been dispatched from Gibraltar, arrived in a very timely fashion as she was to be carrying the survivors so that we could continue with our operational programme once this situation was resolved. Two naval captains, a tug boat skipper and the skippers of both the Yellowstone and the Batouta came together to discuss a way ahead. The biggest concern was Yellowstone's cargo of grain. If that got wet, she would sink like a brick. Batouta's skipper was happy that once separated, she would be able to make her way under her own steam, as she had modern watertight compartments and doorways, and she had counter-flooded her stern to lift the damaged bow out of the water; obviously, this had lifted Yellowstone slightly. Once all heavy cutting was completed and all survivors had been transferred to the tug, Batouta ran up her engines. After two or three attempts at moving astern, she finally broke free of Yellowstone and with her bulbous bow clear of the waterline, she began her onward journey.

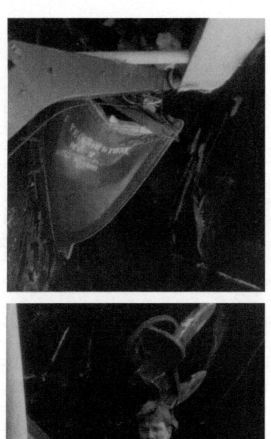

The author amongst the carnage onboard SS Yellowstone

S.S Yellowstone sinks and is gone

Yellowstone began to sink by the stern almost immediately, and, after a few short moments, she was gone beneath the waves. There was nothing left to remind us of what had just happened; it was quite eerie. By now, the weather was deteriorating and the sea state grew to storm levels. The dead and injured were on their way back to Gibraltar, as were survivors by tug. Over the next few hours, the weather deteriorated quite dramatically and we received a radio call from the tug to say that she needed urgent assistance as she was top-heavy and unsafe in these weather conditions. We made our way at best speed towards her position which meant a few uncomfortable hours, given the sea state. Before our arrival, the captain discussed with his senior officers how best we could help. It was totally unsafe to fly our helicopter in these conditions so it was decided to transfer the survivors from the earlier collision to us by sea boat. There is a calculated risk in transferring personnel this way and in these conditions, which is something I raised when the captain asked if I would cox the boat, even though I wasn't on watch. I naturally agreed and said it felt like unfinished business. I asked if I might pick my own crew as I needed men who were trustworthy and level-headed, and needless to say, this was granted. One thing I did say to the skipper was that given the conditions, I might end up losing the boat, particularly after he explained how he wanted it done. Once on scene, the skipper would place the warship across the sea, offering some protection and shelter from the elements, then the tug would move as close to the sea boat as possible, allowing personnel to drop into our sea boat before we attempted to get to Aurora and disembark them. We strapped rattan fenders horizontally on either side of the sea boat; these are like cushions that are normally used vertically to reduce damage when berthing. Our ship lowered cargo netting down our port side to enable survivors to climb out of the sea boat and the tug lowered cargo netting down her starboard side to allow them to climb down.

On our arrival on scene, there were twenty-foot waves so I was sandwiched between a warship and a tug that was going up twenty feet at a time, but as she was going up, so I was going down twenty feet meaning she was forty feet above me. The idea was that as she came down to meet me, survivors would drop into my boat as they couldn't possibly climb in.

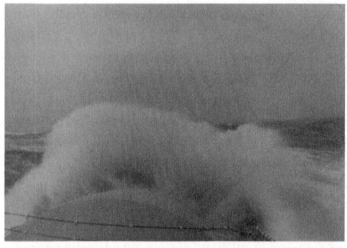

Pretty rough for a sea boat transfer

Any mariner will tell you that this is fraught. It was pitch black in a worsening storm and there would be no controlled access or egress from tug to sea boat, or sea boat to warship. We anticipated a few broken bones in the process and maybe even losing one or two over the side, but as we weren't in a position to recover them, we hoped this wouldn't be the case. When I brought up these very points before launching, the captain said, "Do what you can; it's all you can do". My crew and I had specialist life jackets on, and so, even though we were half expecting to end up in the ocean, we weren't too concerned. Every time the tug went up on the crest of a wave, it came down very hard on my rattan fenders, effectively trying to capsize my boat. As the tug came down, five or six survivors would drop into my boat. The tug manoeuvred away from us and Aurora got as close as she could. When we travelled up on a wave, the survivors grabbed the cargo net as high as they could. We went down and left them holding on, where they were assisted on board. Aurora then moved away from us, but keeping us in the lee of the weather, we repeated the process until all survivors were transferred to Aurora.

Along with everything else, we were totally unaware that we had attracted some marine visitors that were shadowing our every trip - sharks! I later found out that a young officer had pointed out to the captain that we were being followed by a shiver of sharks and they had probably been attracted by blood from myself, from a hand injury sustained in the boat, or from the survivors, some of whom were bleeding. The skipper, with a stiff upper lip, told the young officer to go away and say nothing! He went on to say that the coxswain and crew had enough to think about without bothering them. I am actually glad they said nothing as we reasonably expected to go into the water at some point.

Once all transfers were over and our sea boat was recovered, we were instructed to go to the bridge. The captain had a large shot of rum for each of the crew and nothing but praise for the job that we had done, which was very nice. The Master of the SS Yellowstone was one of the survivors whom we had transferred and he spoke to the captain, saying that in all his years in the

Merchant Marine, he had never seen such fine seamanship and boat-handling skills as he had witnessed on that night and under such extreme conditions.

A few weeks later, the captain called me to his cabin and showed me a letter that he had received which was from the Master of the Yellowstone, and he thanked us formally for saving his and his fellow shipmates' lives. This was a lovely thing and it made me feel ten feet tall. Ordinarily, this would be the end of the story, but unbeknown to me, the captain had forwarded my name for my conduct as being over and above. I was later awarded a Mention in Dispatches, presented with The Queen's Commendation for Bravery, and issued the Bronze Oak Leaf. By the Queen's order, my name was published in the London Gazette on the first of May 1979. These accolades were bestowed upon me with my family present at H.M.S. Excellent in Portsmouth at ceremonial divisions on the very same day.

CHAPTER 6
GALVESTON

On my first ship as a Petty Officer, I was blessed with a great deployment to the Eastern States of America, the Caribbean, and Central and South America. I want to tell the story of my visit to Galveston in Texas. Galveston hadn't had a British warship visit for nearly twenty years and so this was to be a very high-profile visit. Our American liaison officer had flown ahead of the ship in order to assist in the build-up to the visit. Diplomatic clearance had already been granted and our liaison officer was working quite closely with the office of the mayor. The mayor was the first lady mayor in Galveston's history, and, by all accounts, she was wonderful to work with, as she also felt the importance of the upcoming visit. Now, the job of the liaison officer is to raise the profile of the visit as much as possible. It usually involves television and radio interviews, visits to local newspapers, and any businesses that might be interested for commercial reasons or otherwise.

Whilst all the activity was happening ashore, H.M.S. Arrow was preparing herself out at sea. Anything that could be painted, was. The ship was scrubbed from top to bottom, and all brightwork was highly polished. All weapons had their ceremonial tampions fitted, which are ceremonial covers. The ship's helicopter was moved out of its hangar and onto the flight deck where it was spruced up. Every sailor prepared his white uniform, some for the first time, and freshly whitened shoes were drying off all over the ship in readiness for going into the Island of Galveston. And so, the time for entering harbour drew close. As the Petty officer of the cable deck, I was responsible for the high-profile job of ensuring there was an anchor always ready to drop in case of emergency and I was also responsible for securing the front end of the ship when berthing.

My team and I went about our seamanship duties in our normal professional and efficient manner, removing slips and readying both cable and berthing ropes. Suddenly, I was approached by the new forecastle officer who had just appeared on deck, and he told me that he was the person in charge and that any decisions should go through him. I pointed out to him that my crew and myself knew what we were doing and, as things happened quickly on the cable deck, it might be sensible to allow us to work the deck. I also pointed out that arriving at this point is very late in proceedings and that the captain wouldn't be happy with his late arrival. Not one to be told, this new and very inexperienced officer decided against my advice and reiterated that he was the one to make the decisions. I instructed my team to take their instructions from the new 'boss' and effectively took a back seat. From very early on, a few things came to light. Firstly, he didn't really understand how the cable deck worked, and, on two or three occasions, I stepped in just to keep it safe. Procedurally, he didn't understand the sequence of events that needed to take place in order to ready an anchor. I stood on his shoulder trying to assist him but he wouldn't be told. Bear in mind that all this was going on in full view of the bridge, and, more particularly, the captain. As a point of clarity, the forecastle officer's job is to man the communications headset and relay any messages from the bridge. He must stand back from working the deck otherwise he cannot oversee safety which is his other job. By now, the captain had obviously seen enough and summoned the young officer to the bridge. After a few short moments, the officer returned and asked if I would take charge of the forecastle. He also apologised to me personally and then manned the communications headset. Whilst I don't know exactly what was said on the bridge, he returned looking like the stereotypical scolded schoolboy. After this unsavoury start to our working relationship, we built up a good professional rapport that lasted for the duration of my time on board.

On the jetty, they had rigged a small grandstand which, by now, was full of happy families and folk just wanting to be part of the occasion. In true American over-the-top style, they had laid on a massive welcome on the jetty. Television cameras from two local and one national station were in attendance, as was local radio. A marching band from the local college was playing away and practising their tunes, a troop of baton twirlers was working quite closely with the marching band, and, to keep all the red-blooded sailors happy, a team of cheerleaders was practising their skills. Stalls selling all sorts of local food, and some not so local, were in abundance, there was piped music for when the band was not playing and right in the middle was the raised podium where the Lady Mayor waited in earnest.

Meanwhile, out at sea, the captain had decided not to accept berthing assistance from local tugs, which is the norm, but to do things his own way. This was not entirely surprising as he had always been a very independent person. Type 21 Frigates, of which Arrow was one, have a very special set of propellers which are called variable pitch propellers. They differ in that a conventional propeller on a prop shaft spins clockwise to go forward, and to go astern, it has to be slowed down to a stop and then run in the opposite direction, which takes time and a greater distance. Variable pitch props, whilst spinning clockwise, only need to have the pitch altered to give it immediate stern power with no slowing down of the prop shaft, thus stopping the ship from greater speeds much more quickly.

As we ran down towards the berth at speed, you could hear the band playing and sense the expectation;

it was palpable. Baton twirlers were twirling, cheerleaders were 'cheerleading', and there was a real sense of occasion. The captain on the bridge roof was waving and the ship's company looked immaculate. What could possibly go wrong? Misjudging his position, the skipper took us too close to the jetty and as we arrived at the berthing point, we were going far too fast. The stern of the ship went underneath the berth and started ripping out our guardrail stanchions. The superstructure started to scrape along the jetty ripping out safety posts and chains in the process. Our chaps moved quickly back away from danger and people on the jetty were running away from the ship which was, by now, rapidly slowing down. Our helicopter got perilously close to a large jetty structure but thankfully made no contact.

As the ship came to an abrupt stop, to coin an expression, 'the band played on'. With cameras rolling and everyone watching, we probably couldn't have had a worse start to a visit. Welcome to Galveston, the Royal Navy is here. After announcing our arrival in the most public of ways, we settled down to what would turn out to be a really great visit.

On the first night out with all the ceremonial completed, four of us from the mess decided to take a walk ashore. Expecting a late night and the possibility of going clubbing, we dressed accordingly, as the Americans are usually quite strict about dress codes. Our first 'port of call', which ended up being our last, was the very posh

'Hotel Galvez and Spa, a very grand-looking place with two main bars and, most importantly, a nightclub; this looked like just what we were after so in we went. The place didn't disappoint; it was very grand indeed. The only downside was the fact that it was very quiet with hardly anyone in the bar. The barman told us that it was early yet and that things picked up from about ten onwards. We ordered a round of drinks and made our way to a table.

A voice called out from across the room, 'Hey, are you British sailors from that warship?' We naturally concurred and expected a barrage of abuse based on our entry. The abuse never came; in fact, what came was the offer of a round of drinks, in a very deep Texan brawl, on them. Never knowingly missing an opportunity, we asked if we could join them and moved tables. So, here we were, four well-dressed clean-cut sailors looking immaculate and smelling of Brut and Denim, sat drinking with two older-looking men with very long beards, long leather coats (indoors), and with deep southern accents. One of our foursome was quite animated as he recognised the two gents - they were two-thirds of the rock band ZZ-Top, namely Dusty Hill and Billy Gibbons. They had had numerous hits over a long career including songs like 'Eliminator', 'Legs', and 'Sharp Dressed Man'. Wow, we were in the company of rock royalty!

So now all fully aware of who these two gents were, we began chasing shots with them. As I recall, this was their idea, as they fancied themselves to drink us under the table. Never being too shy to step up to the challenge, and remembering the Royal Navy's reputation was at stake, we began a crazy few hours of mindless alcohol abuse. As the evening wore on, we ended up dancing on the tables and singing anything we could to try and match them. I think it would be fair to say that they won that part of the competition, but the drinking challenge was another issue. When, eventually, Billy Gibbons, I think it was, fell off his table and came crashing down, they conceded that we won the shooting competition. The fall ended proceedings and they left for their respective rooms as they were staying at the hotel. By now, the club had opened but we were extremely socially confused so we only lasted a short while before we made our way back on board for a good sleep.

There seemed to be a trend of alcohol abuse running through our stay in Galveston and the final part of my story begins on day two. Whilst at the Hotel Galvez nightclub the previous night, and unbeknown to me, I had given a young lady my personal details. Imagine my surprise when I got a telephone call from Gina, whilst on board. We made a date and met after work, and for the rest of our time there, we got on famously. On one of the evenings, Gina asked if I was happy to make up a foursome with her girlfriend Sam and Sam's boyfriend Steve. I of course agreed and we decided to have a Mexican meal out and then go bopping.

Now, American women, I can deal with but American men always seem to have a chip on their shoulders. Steve turned out to be no different; he was very self-centred, arrogant and fiercely competitive. In conversation, anything that I had done, he had done twice. Anything I had, he had two of; you know the sort. Anyway, after a lovely meal and no shortage of Margaritas, we slipped through to the in-house club for more drinks. This is where Steve challenged me, for no obvious reason, to a drinking challenge. "We'll shoot the worm," he said, and he ordered some drinks, one for me and one for him. Gina warned me about what to expect, as I think he was getting to her as well. Two miniature bottles of Tequila Gold turned up, each with a large grub in it, which is what the Americans call a worm. Now I drink and am fond of Tequila, so that held no fear for me, but the worm was something else. Steve said that you had to drink the tequila down and swallow the worm, so off he went. After successfully downing his drink, I tried to think about how to put him in his place. So, I drank half the Tequila and put the worm on my tongue, I then bit the worm in half releasing lots of greenish-yellow goo into my mouth, which I showed off. I then swallowed half the worm and then washed the other half down with the rest of the Tequila. His face was a picture and he conceded defeat, which felt great. What didn't feel great was the feeling of impending sickness growing in my stomach. The worm tasted absolutely foul and was trying to make an exit. Determined not to lose face, I carried on drinking my Margarita for a good five minutes or so before excusing myself and going to the gents. There, the inevitable happened, but after quickly cleaning up, I returned and nobody was any the wiser.

CHAPTER 7
ANTIGUA - A PERMANENT
REMINDER

During a tour of the Caribbean in the early 1980s, HMS Arrow was fortunate enough to be sent to the beautiful island of Antigua. Now there are four things that matter in Antigua; reggae, rum, cricket, and sailing, but not necessarily in that order. Day one in any port follows a pretty standard format. Store ship, official visits, defect repairs, and a ceremonial cocktail party for local politicians, dignitaries, businessmen, and anyone else that can blag a ticket. I usually stay on board until eight o clock on the first day alongside, as there is a high level of ceremonial, culminating in firing a volley of blanks to conclude the cocktail party, and I am responsible for both the guard and the ceremonial training.

So then, on the first full day, a walk into the capital of St. John's was on the agenda. I suppose there were about six of us who set out that morning and on our way into town, we came across what looked like a field filled with locals who were eating, drinking, and smoking who knows what. There must have been well over a thousand people; some were picnicking on blankets, lots of youngsters were playing, reggae music rang out everywhere, particularly Bob Marley, and occasionally, you could hear cricket commentary. Quite obviously, we were attracted to and intrigued by what was going on, so we walked in through a wide-open access to join the party. It was at this point that we realised we were gate-crashing a cricket match. The field that we were now in was on one side of a cricket field, away from the central area which had a small grandstand on it, but with a great view of the game. We made our way towards a makeshift shack where we could buy the local 'Wadadli' beer or the national drink of rum punch. We bought a round of drinks and asked the chap selling the beer who was playing. What we had stumbled upon was an international game between Clive Lloyd's West Indies and Ian Botham's England. What a result! We stayed and partied all day long with the local cricket fans, drinking beer and rum and listening to reggae. Lunch was rum and jerk chicken, which I highly recommend. Needless to say, we never made it into St. John's that day. I heard that the series was won by the West Indies 2-0, which seemed to be the catalyst for a four or five-day party on the island.

Early the next morning, we had booked taxis to take us to a resort called 'The Jolly Beach Resort and Spa', south and west of St. John's. We had heard great things about this place but it was a little too far to walk. On our arrival at the resort, we paid to use the facilities, grabbed some towels, and headed for the pool and beach, which were alongside one another. Early it might have been but never too early to start, so we ordered drinks and had them delivered to the pool-side. Having had more than enough rum over the last few days, I opted for my favourite, gin and tonic. One led to two, two led to three, and so on. Swimming in the beautiful sea, and occasionally in the pool, was idyllic. We ate at the hotel and it was fantastic, and then back to pick up where we'd left off. I am not proud of the fact that I got very drunk, but I did. I am fortunate that I can hold my drink well and rarely get sick or punchy but we had an awful lot to drink on this particular day.

All good things come to an end and so we organised taxis back to the ship as it was getting quite late. One of our crowd had a really great idea as we arrived on the jetty and suggested that we continue the party in the mess on board.

So, now back in the mess, we continued where we had left off at the hotel, drinking. The evening spilled very easily into the night and into the wee small hours and then somebody decided it was time for party pieces. Party pieces are something unique to that individual, a skill or a trick that they can do, usually when they are drunk. I was about as drunk as it is possible to get without collapsing, but it was now my turn and so I rose to the occasion. I grabbed a sailmaker's darning needle, which is similar to an ordinary needle but about three inches long and triangular through its length, a very sturdy needle used for repairing canvas. I placed the needle against my elbow joint on the inside of my arm so that half the needle was above the joint and half was below the joint. I then folded my arm closed, raising my wrist to my shoulder. This causes the needle to sit in a pocket of skin and rarely even breaks the skin. If it should break the skin, which occasionally happens, then it's no big deal as it's just like getting a pinprick. Once I got the required response from the lads, I began to open my arm, when I felt a more prominent than usual prod from the needle. The needle had actually pierced my lower arm and had gone in about two-thirds of its length! Realising that this wasn't right, but giving the lads a laugh in the process, I attempted to remove the needle. Making a big mistake that I blame on drink, I got things horribly wrong. Instead of just holding my arm position where it was and grabbing the eye of the needle, I straightened my arm first and watched the needle disappear beneath the surface with not so much as a drop of blood to show where it had been! Now I was looking at my arm in shock while the lads were having a laugh at my expense. After the initial responses to what had just occurred, there was a general consensus that we needed to report this to the Doc.

Now, the "Doc", as we lovingly call him, is actually a male nurse who looks after a small sickbay on board and whose duties would normally include issuing medication, cleaning up grazes, administering injections, and minor injury repairs, including stitches, when necessary. Our Doc was called George, and he was from the North-East. George didn't like being woken up at night without good reason. Here were a dozen or so very drunken sailors trying to convince George that I really did have a sailmaker's needle somewhere inside my arm.

After eventually convincing George that what we were telling him was true - perhaps the fact that after a day on the beach I was still as white as a ghost may have convinced him - he conceded that there was indeed a need for his intervention. After getting out of his bunk, George dragged everyone to the Quarterdeck to begin collecting the mobile x-ray equipment that lived in about ten armoured suitcases in the medical store underneath the weather decks. After about an hour, we had everything in the sickbay and George began assembling the kit. At this point, Doc sent everyone off to bed as it was extremely late and to be fair, a dozen drunken sailors would be more of a hindrance than a help. Once assembled, Doc placed my arm on the operating table with my left elbow in contact with the table and my left-hand palm up. He took a couple of x-rays and there was the obligatory wait. Nothing to see. George then moved my arm further down the table effectively looking further up the arm. Eureka, this time Doc could see the needle! I felt an immediate sense of relief as I was beginning to doubt myself as to whether it had happened or not. The next step was surgery, right here and right now under a local.

George made an incision about an inch long but found nothing. He then adjusted my position and made a second incision, again about an inch long and about an inch from the first but still nothing. At this stage, I need to point out that as a nurse, he can only go so far with his incisions and certainly cannot go deep. George was a proud individual and was determined not to be beaten by this problem so he re-thought what he was doing and then decided to turn my arm through ninety degrees and x-ray the site. This course of action paid dividends, as he was not only able to see exactly where the needle was but also how deep it was and it was right in the centre of my arm. Too deep for George to tackle, he went about giving me six stitches in each incision and had me sleep in the sickbay for what was left of the night.

The next morning, George was on the radio phone to Royal Naval Hospital Haslar, in Portsmouth, UK. The advice from RNH Haslar was to immobilise the arm with a sling, to confine me to the mess, and to put me on a course of antibiotics to clear or avoid any infection. As we were sailing for the UK the next day, and ordinarily a trip across the Atlantic takes about ten to twelve days, the Naval Hospital staff were happy to wait until our arrival to see me.

So, now looking at my 'war-wound', I began to realise that I had probably got a more permanent reminder of a great time in Antigua than I had wanted, and, it wasn't over yet. On our arrival back in 'dear old Blighty', George escorted me to the local Naval Hospital, which was Stonehouse. They carried out a detailed examination and took some slightly more professional x-rays. Additionally, the nurse removed my stitches. After the mandatory wait, the doctor called me and George into his office. After congratulating George on his needle-work, no pun intended, he explained to me that there are lots of people walking around with bits of metal inside them, and as long as there was no pain and no sign of infection, the best course of action would be to do nothing. I had no trouble accepting his decision and couldn't wait to get back to normal.

I'm afraid normal didn't last for very long. Only a week or so later, I was at my local, playing competitive pool when I screwed a shot. For those that don't play, this is when you spin the cue on striking the ball in order to make the cue ball do something different. I screamed out in pain as I struck the ball, with what felt like an electrical bolt going through my left arm. I immediately dropped the cue and quickly realised that I had no use of my middle and ring fingers; they wouldn't budge. Unbeknown to me, what had happened was that the needle in my arm had snapped in half and the lower half was sitting against the nerves that operated the two fingers. After a short time spent at the hospital, an operation was arranged for me to have the needle removed at the Naval Hospital the next day. I arrived under escort, poor old George, at RNH ready for my operation, which was to be done under general anaesthetic. I'm not one to be picky, but once I had been processed and put on the ward, I was given my pre-med. During this time, a nurse came to my bed and drew a black arrow in pen on my arm and then put iodine on the entire site. The reason I mentioned being picky is that the nurse had marked up my right arm, and, in my semi-conscious state, I wasn't sure whether this was right or not. I already had two very distinctive scars on my left arm as a result of the visit to Antigua and I didn't need anymore. Just before I went into theatre, the doctor had a look at my notes and the marks on my right arm were moved to the left arm!

Finally, I woke up with a large well-padded bandage on the correct arm. Both halves of the needle had been removed and I now had a much larger scar, although as yet unseen. On the bedside unit next to my bed was a small specimen jar which I still have to this day. In it are the two halves of the needle and on it were the words 'One party trick, don't do it again', which I haven't since.

CHAPTER 8
JUNGLE TRAINING

Every so often, there is a need for a British warship to be stationed in the Caribbean, and this commitment is called West Indies Guardship or W.I.G.S. The operational excuse for being there is to assist those islands loyal to the crown with their naval training, but we would also support any disaster relief that may be necessary. The real reason, I suspect, is so that sailors can enjoy what the Caribbean has to offer! During one of these many patrols, we were dispatched to Belize in Central America. Upon our arrival, our Ship's Internal Security platoon consisting of one Officer, one Senior Non-Commissioned Officer, and thirty men, moved ashore to carry out jungle training with the resident battalion, which in this case was the Parachute Regiment. In exchange for our thirty-two men being ashore and training with the Army, we welcomed thirty-two soldiers on board for naval training. We call this an exchange visit and each would fill one another's shoes for a week or so.

Once we had disembarked our team, we were met on the jetty by a Sergeant from the Parachute Regiment. We each carried a backpack with all the necessary clothing and what we needed to survive five days in the jungle. We also carried three days' worth of ration packs and our personal weapon. We embarked on a three-tonner lorry and were whisked off to a camp known as 'Holdfast', which is right on the edge of the jungle and in the middle of nowhere. Upon our arrival, we were separated, the Officer to the Officers' mess, me to the Warrant Officer and Senior Non-Commissioned Officers' Mess, and the lads to the NAAFI, the social hub for the junior ranks. The next twelve hours were a blur of food, rum, beer, and port. After a crazy night of being welcomed and trying to decide who could outdrink who, we met on the parade square the next morning for briefing, before setting off into the Belizean jungle. The lorries took us as far as they were able but we disembarked and made our way on foot for the last couple of miles or so.

When we arrived in the dense bush, we set our gear down and were given a safety brief by the corporal in charge. He showed us the immediate area and where each of our three rifle sections would be making camp. Myself and the 'boss' were put in an adjacent area. The next few hours consisted of demonstrations on things like how to rig a latrine, or toilet, how to keep clean and dry, how to build a bivouac or bed, and what you can and can't eat or drink. After the initial briefings, the corporal allowed everyone to get on with making camp. This was also the time that I realised that things were not going to be as smooth as they should be. The corporal invited the boss and myself to go around the sites with him to troubleshoot any issues.

On our arrival at the first campsite, the lads were finishing off their bivouacs and starting to put some food together. Bear in mind that they should only be carrying a list of items that are strictly controlled and the only food they should have is their ration packs which measure roughly 20cms square. One of the lads was holding and eating from a catering-size tin of peaches which he had 'acquired' from the catering office whilst on board ship and had subsequently smuggled ashore. As soon as the corporal saw the very large tin, he snapped at the lad and asked him where he had gotten the tin from. The response he got was, "From my ration pack, Corporal". The corporal turned to leave and then the penny dropped; the tin couldn't possibly fit in a ration pack. He smiled realising that the lad had got one up on him. At this point, I felt compelled to explain to the corporal that these were sailors and not soldiers and whilst their heart was in the right place, they would never make infantrymen.

The next day began very early with someone screaming! Now, the jungle isn't the quietest of places but this was way over and above. Nobody would move, in fear, I think. Sailors are strange creatures; they are the salt of the earth, but they have a way of making life easier for themselves by doing things their own way, rather than the way they have been shown or taught. So, yesterday's demonstration on how to build a bivouac between two strong trees hadn't fully sunk in with everyone. A bivouac is like a hammock strung between two strong points and up from the ground; this is done so that you don't get any unwelcome visitors through the night. Additionally, you rig a line above your 'bivvy' to hold a mosquito net that you tuck underneath yourself when you climb in to sleep. The noise that we all heard earlier was the result of 'Ossie' cutting corners on the choice of trees to support his bivvy - so small was the tree that it couldn't hold his weight and the foot of his bivvy collapsed. This had happened much earlier in the night than the screaming and we subsequently found out why. When his bivvy collapsed, Ossie found it really quite comfortable and so he decided not to bother getting up and fixing it. Obviously, Ossie had paid lip service to not only the bivvy brief but also the brief about no littering in the jungle, as that might also invite unwanted guests. Ossie had cleared out half the sweets and chocolate bars from our onboard NAAFI and was carrying them with him. He had sweets before retiring and discarded the wrappers right underneath his bivvy, by kicking them under some leaves and undergrowth. The screaming we all heard was Ossie reacting to hundreds of soldier ants, having been attracted by his sweet wrappers, which were now crawling all over him. No serious damage was done but I think lessons were learned.

Another day in the jungle came with today's focus on survival techniques. During the latter part of the afternoon and fairly close to sunset, the corporal pulled everybody together in a clearing and began a presentation on navigating in the bush and how to move around safely. He covered the more obvious use of the sun and of the moon and stars, but also the use of foliage and moss and animal tracks among other things. Like everybody else, I had listened to what he had to say and felt it had been worthwhile, but then he started pairing people up. I had alarm bells ringing and asked him what he was intending to do. He told me that he had picked out a route through the intense bush, which was about two miles long, and after last light, he intended to send pairs out at intervals through the bush, to practise what they had just learned. He reckoned two miles at night would take them through to first light, where we would meet them. The boss and I suggested that this wasn't such a good idea as we would probably never see them again and there were only four safety staff to oversee this exercise. The corporal was quite surprised and slightly annoyed at what we had said, so he randomly picked out sailors and questioned them on the instruction that they had just been given. Almost without exception, they hadn't taken in anything of importance, and there were varying degrees of having taken anything in at all that might help them on a night exercise! The night navigation exercise was cancelled due to a genuine fear of losing sailors permanently. When we settled down to eat our last ration pack that evening, I tried to explain that the lads weren't just trying to be awkward for the sake of it, but that this was a bit of a jolly for them and a chance to get off the ship. I went on to reiterate that they were hard-working experts in their own respective fields, but were used to three square meals a day, with a hot shower and a warm bed to retire to.

Partially conceding defeat, the corporal instructed his team to break out the beer from the store tent, and instead of night navigation, we found something that the lads could do well - drink. So, the next few hours were spent around the fire we had built, drinking beer and putting the world to rights. As the evening was drawing to a close, there was a strange visual effect to the left of our campsite which looked like a flag being waved at ground level, almost like water flowing. The staff told us that it was bird-eating spiders migrating, and that they had been drawn to the flames, but that they wouldn't harm us. Of course, we totally ignored what they said. Maybe we aren't cut out to be infantrymen but we are not that gullible; who'd ever heard of bird-eating spiders? One of the lads threw an empty can towards the strange sight and it separated immediately. It was exactly as they told us, hundreds of bird-eating spiders on the move, and these things really are as big as your hand. This sort of finished the party off, and suddenly, everyone was keen to get into the sanctuary of their bivvies. The corporal reminded everyone about personal checks and hygiene before they got their heads down. He seemed quite mellow in himself that evening, but to this day, I don't know whether it was the beer or the satisfaction of finally getting the lads to listen and take things more seriously. Next morning, when I awoke, I was about to put my boots on and go for a wash, however, grabbing my boots from the high point that I had hung them from, one seemed a little heavier than it should be. So, remembering the brief, I didn't put my hand inside to pull out the tongue but banged it very firmly upside down. Suddenly, a large land crab crawled out of my boot and scuttled off. I was slightly shaken but very happy that I hadn't just put my hand inside, as I have been told that they have quite a bite.

Having now run out of food, three-tonner lorries brought fresh victuals to the clearing where we had disembarked from, so we made our way under supervision to the disembarkation point and retrieved the stores from the lorries. Once back at camp, we stowed everything in the stores' tent but we didn't know what to do with the forty or so live chickens that were in makeshift cages. Our brief was that these chickens would make up the substance of that evening's meal. A field kitchen was set up ready to give a presentation on catching, killing, preparing, and eating your food, to be given later that day.

The corporal, the boss and myself were taken away from the campsite for a field meeting and were gone for about two hours. On our return, none of us could quite believe what we were seeing. Rather than killing the chickens with a view to cleaning and preparing them for eating, the lads had let the chickens out of their cages, named them, and adopted one each! Each person has to carry spare boot laces as part of their emergency kit and these had been utilised as leads for the chickens. The newly named chickens were being led around the campsite by their newly adopted 'parents'. The lads didn't have the heart to kill the chickens and even though the corporal told them that they would go hungry, they still wouldn't, as unbeknown to everybody, they had topped up at our onboard NAAFI with everything from Pot Noodles to Oxo cubes and vegetable soup to tinned tuna prior to coming ashore.

Once again, the corporal wasn't impressed, and so he began the presentation in earnest. He grabbed a chicken, took it to the field table, and, with a large machete, beheaded it. Blood squirted everywhere and the chicken's nervous system kept it moving for quite some time. The mood was quite solemn among the sailors but maybe for the first time, there was a realisation that this was serious training with fun bits rather than fun training with serious bits. With the mood much more focused on the job in hand, the safety team showed us how to strip a chicken and what was edible and what wasn't. After having been shown how to clean and prep food ready for cooking, we moved on to how to catch it in the first place. I think this would all have happened in a slightly different sequence if the corporal hadn't 'lost it' at the beginning. We moved on to identifying animal runs and where best to establish traps and snares. We were also shown how to catch animals of differing sizes. Popular with the lads was the noose. A noose is made up of vegetation around the site of the trap. The idea is that the noose is placed on the animal's run at a height that would snag the animal at head height and its forward momentum would spring the noose and catch the animal. Obviously, depending on the animal that you are trying to catch, will depend on how robust the snare needs to be.

The Lads

Anyone for chicken?

The author jungle training in Belize

The teams were then split up, some going back to camp for their evening meal and some waiting and watching the traps. After a ridiculously long period of inactivity, the safety team decided to help things along by encouraging the sailors to walk their now fully adopted pets into the snares. Reluctance is a word that springs to mind, but reluctantly, they began to coax their chickens into the traps. I heard one of our team, a guy nick-named Blood, calling out to his chicken, "Come on, Betsy, come on, Betsy." Betsy was almost dragged into the trap until it sprung, but the poor chicken was far too heavy for the noose around her neck, her neck went up but her feet stayed on the ground, poor thing. After much laughter, the others started following suit, so the exercise wasn't a complete waste of time.

Whilst the team at the traps continued to monitor them in the hope of catching something other than a chicken, the corporal, the boss and myself made our way back towards the main campsite. The intention was for us to eat along with those back at camp and then swap those who had eaten with those at the traps so that they might eat. Bear in mind that these are sailors who have no survival skills whatsoever. They were only in possession of a now-dead chicken, water, salt plus any remnants from their ration packs. Additionally, there were a few fresh (ish) vegetables for their use, so they were not expected to produce anything other than very basic food to eat. Well, imagine our surprise as we approached the campsite where we could smell many different things being cooked, and very nice it smelled too. Then, as we got closer, we could hear dialogue. "Hey, Spike, have you got any garlic left?" "Yeah, but it will cost you an Oxo," came the reply. Then we heard, "Is there any chicken soup left in the pot?" "Yes, mate, help yourself." "How's the spit roast going, Paddy?" was the last thing we heard before we entered the campsite.

Paddy had built a very basic but quite brilliant spit roast that he was cranking, to ensure his chicken was properly cooked; he was even basting it as he went along. There was cock au vin, chicken curry, and chicken chasseur; this wasn't a campsite in the middle of the Belizean jungle, this was a Michelin-starred kitchen that MasterChef would have been proud of!

I felt a massive sense of pride at this point that these sailors could surpass all expectations and produce so much from so little. The corporal was gob-smacked and said that he hadn't seen anything like it in his entire career. Along with an immense sense of pride, I was seeing the lighter side of things. Who, for example, would expect to find a spit roast in the bush? What made things more endearing was that everyone pooled their food 'banquet-style' and we ate extremely well with the lads. I did have a slightly sobering thought during dinner - if the lads had been carrying all these extra victuals and goodness knows what else, I wondered what kit they had chosen to leave on board. I never asked!

After another noisy sleep under the stars, it was up for a wash and some breakfast before a day of infantry training. Up first was close-quarter combat, as the Army call it, or bayonet drills as we sailors called it. One of the safety team had dressed fully for combat and had camouflaged himself, his webbing and his equipment ready for battle. The staff had rigged a gallows-type arrangement with a dummy hanging from it. There was also a medicine ball hanging from the upper frame and a large sandbag at the base of the frame. So, first, by way of a demonstration, the corporal ordered the soldier, "On guard!" The soldier screamed, "arrrgh!" very loudly and adopted the on-guard position, which meant he was leaning forward aggressively and pointing his rifle at the gallows. It was obvious that these were specialist skills and not the time for making fun, so everyone put their serious heads on and responded to the demonstration. The corporal then ordered, "Advance!" The soldier then advanced, growling very loudly as he did so, then he plunged his bayonet into the hanging dummy, twisted it and withdrew it. He then used the butt of his rifle to strike the medicine ball, again with a loud audible "arrgh". He stuck his bayonet into the sandbag before placing his foot on the sandbag and withdrawing the bayonet, before taking a step to his left and adopting an on-guard position again, whilst all of the time making a very aggressive "arrgh" sound.

Okay, demonstration over and time for the Royal Navy to have a go. First up was Jock, and, although sequentially correct, it lacked any real conviction and there was certainly no aggressive noise from him. Next up was better, again with a little more noise and aggression, and so things got better as the day went on. By now, all the corporal wanted to see an improvement on was noise and aggression. There were one or two individuals that really didn't fancy getting involved but this is compulsory training and not optional, so they were motivated.

Banjo was up next and so he took the rifle from the soldier and waited. The corporal ordered, "On guard!" and with a bit of a grunt, Banjo did as he was ordered. His on-guard position was good but he showed little aggression. The corporal then ordered, "Advance!" Banjo moved forward aggressively and plunged the bayonet into the dummy, he then twisted it and withdrew it, before using his rifle butt to strike the medicine ball at the top of the frame. He then took a step back and placed his foot on the large sandbag at the base of the gallows before plunging his bayonet through his own foot and into the large sandbag, pinning his foot in the process! For the first time, he let out an almighty scream as he realised what he had done. Banjo fell backwards onto the floor whilst still pinned and was screaming in agony. The corporal rushed forward to render assistance and initial first aid and thirty sailors burst into laughter at what they were witnessing. Needless to say, the exercise was stopped so that we could get a helicopter from 'Holdfast' to casevac Banjo to the field hospital. Casevac is a casualty evacuation. A point to note is that Banjo made a full recovery, and, whilst in hospital for three days, he got all the luxuries that you might expect, like three square meals a day, a hot shower, and a nice clean bed. Don't feel too sorry for him.

During my first visit to the Belizean jungle some years earlier, my then Petty Officer instructed the entire platoon not to eat the sweets that come in the ration packs. He explained that all would become clear when we left the jungle. In keeping with tradition, I had requested that my team saved the sweets from their ration packs and that the reason why would become evident when we left the jungle. So, departure day came with all the packing and subsequent loading of the trucks. Once organised, we began our slow journey to Holdfast camp. As we exited the jungle, we came across the small indigenous villages that are scattered around, and, to everyone's surprise, young children came running towards the lorries from all directions. The reason for hanging onto the sweets was now apparent and we began throwing them to the youngsters who were chasing after the trucks. This has become something of a tradition on these visits to Belize and the children seem to know that when the lorries leave the jungle, there will be sweets for all. The look on their young faces made hanging onto the sweets so worthwhile.

CHAPTER 9
HMS ACTIVE

In 1990, HMS Active acted as Royal guardship for the Royal Yacht Britannia and had a lovely run down the West Coast of Africa. The Prince and Princess of Wales were resident on board the Yacht and we were to meet them in Gibraltar. Prior to the Royal Yacht arriving in Gibraltar, we had a chance to practise some rusty skills. This deployment was ceremonial rather than operational although there was quite obviously an operational element to it. Ceremonial Divisions were to go ahead in Gibraltar in readiness for the Royal Couple. We had a couple of rehearsals on the jetty, which included the Royal Marines' Band, and Flag Officer Gibraltar himself was to be the inspecting officer. The date was set and all preparations went ahead in earnest.

A very casual Charles and Diana watching HMS Active
steam past from the Royal Yacht Britannia

Our mess, the Chief Petty Officers' mess, had
arranged a Mess Dinner ashore in a lovely restaurant
on the eve of divisions. This was to let off a bit of steam
prior to a busy period with lots of sea time. Now, military
mess dinners are quite formal functions with lots of eti-
quette and rules to abide by. Fines, usually in the form
of bottles of port, are handed out, even for the slightest
misdemeanour. Silver service is the order of the day and
as long as you follow the President rather than pre-empt-
ing him, you should be okay. The food and service were
superb and we got to a point where ordinarily the Pres

would allow us to ease springs, or go to the toilet. Dave, the Pres, hadn't felt the need for a toilet break so there wasn't one. By now, some mess members were really desperate and prepared to take a chance on a fine, so, one at a time, they slipped under the long table and crawled out at the end and into the toilets. As they returned, they crawled back along under the tables and then discretely re-seated themselves. Apart from ourselves, there were only two other people in the restaurant; an older, distinguished-looking gent who was sitting with a very lovely looking but seemingly much younger lady. Every time one of our team left by the table route, the couple found it funny but didn't let the cat out of the bag. This went on until eventually, Dave eased springs. Once dinner was over, it was cigars, coffee, and some serious drinking way into the night.

Next morning, and with a few woolly heads, it was divisions. Platoons were mustering on the jetty and were being dressed whilst the Royal Marines' band played on. As the ship's ceremonial trainer, I don't fall in with any platoon. I oversee and troubleshoot any issues, of which there were few. It was a beautiful spring morning and we were approaching the time when Flag Officer Gibraltar would arrive. Spot on time, the Admiral arrived and was saluted. Our captain, a very senior captain, escorted him and invited him to inspect the platoons. He started with the Officers' platoon and then moved to the Chief Petty Officers' platoon. Once in front of our platoon, some of our guys recognised him as being the gent in the restaurant the evening before. Flag Officer Gibraltar had witnessed the Chief's mess fall into disarray and get smashed. The Admiral asked where Dave our President was. Conveniently for Dave, our Vice President told the Admiral that he was on board as the Duty Officer. The Admiral was a little disappointed because he had warmed to Dave the night before with the way that he had conducted himself. They had also struck up conversation late in the evening when Dave had tried to chat up his wife! Needless to say, our skipper had no idea about any of this and he didn't seem too impressed. This was when we first realised that Dave was a bit of a party animal and this was to be borne out over the following months.

I think we'll travel to the Gambia on Africa's West Coast for the next story. Our visit here was both successful and productive. Any visit to any port is usually well promoted in order to glean as much interest as possible. All the ceremonial and hospitality efforts encourage support for, and often sales of, British business and goods. Any interest in our arrival can be trebled due to the fact that the Royal Yacht was in attendance and more so because they were carrying Charles and Diana. Now, the Gambia was to be a very busy ceremonial visit with 'ship open to visitors' days, cocktail parties, and embassy and numerous consulate visits. Lots of work for everyone but with beautiful beaches and a thriving hotel scene, our rest and relaxation were well accommodated for.

On one of these many social occasions, the ship was presented with a beautiful African Grey Parrot. It was a lovely present, but how on earth could we look after a parrot on a modern warship? Where would we keep it, how would we feed it, and what would we do if it got ill? Most importantly, we couldn't land it back in the UK without following strict quarantine regulations. We needn't have worried because, in true Dunkirk spirit, the Stokers' Mess stepped in and said that they would look after it. The parrot came with its cage and about a two-week supply of food, which was passed to the Stokers' Mess. Like kids with a new pet, the stokers warmed to the parrot and called him Jack, which is the nickname for sailors, so Jack it was. I think it would be fair to say that the food that came with Jack was hardly touched because the lads took Jack with them to the dining room at meal times and they even produced a rota stating whose duty it was. Jack ate whatever the lads ate; if he liked it, he got more, if he didn't like it, they didn't bother again. Over the next few months, they put together a list of Jack's favourite food. For his part in our 'adoption' of Jack, the ship's Doc, our male nurse, read up what he could on parrots so that he could act as a makeshift vet. Having said that, I don't think he was ever called upon.

African Greys are renowned for their ability to mimic sounds and this wasn't lost on the stokers. As you might expect, they taught Jack to say all sorts with some very X-rated expletives. You could be standing in the supper queue and, from behind, Jack would say "F--- Off" or "You're a prick". Whilst this was all good fun, unbeknown to the stokers, Jack was developing other skills. In a warship, pipes are made over the ship's broadcast system. Wake up is by pipe, go to sleep is by pipe, hands to dinner is by pipe, etcetera. Jack was now repeating these pipes perfectly, to the point where it was hard to differentiate between him and the real thing. Because Jack was a parrot and not officially a member of the Royal Navy, he didn't realise that these pipes were supposed to go out at certain times of the day, and he sounded what he wanted when he wanted to. On numerous occasions, Jack sounded 'call the hands' in the middle of the night. Stokers were getting up and putting lights and radios on before they realised it was Jack and it was only three in the morning. Maybe it was some sort of poetic justice on Jack's part. Jack's wings were clipped so he couldn't fly off, and, as the deployment went on, he became more and more settled, so much so that the stokers were able to take him for short walks ashore when in port. I left HMS Active some two years later and at that point, Jack was still living in the mess square of the Stokers' Mess. I believe that one of the stokers put Jack through quarantine and took him on full-time.

Whilst deployed, we were enjoying some downtime whilst alongside. Amongst the visitors to the Mess were two American ladies from the 'Peace Mission'. The Peace Mission is an American organisation whose aim is to provide charitable support to those most in need. Usually, American students take a year out from studies to join up with the Mission to assist in whatever way they can, and wherever it is. These two girls had chosen the West African coast. The girls had been in the Mess for some time when I came in from training to get a drink of juice. Whilst I was standing behind the bar, I could clearly hear the conversation. One of the two girls was very definitely full of her own self-importance, but her arrogance didn't sit well with someone who was suppos-edly here to help local people. She went on about how they were building bridges for the more cut-off villages so that they would have better access to the freshwater installations that they were engineering. Both girls were very pretty and the lads were attracted like magnets. I think the girls knew this and were playing on it a little bit. Hanging on the walls of our Mess were pictures of the ship firing off her weapon systems. That last sentence might seem a little left of centre but bear with me. The young lady with the ego caught my eye and she made a bee-line towards me. She said, "Hi, my name is Chrissy, and what do you do?" I politely responded and told her my name; I then said, "You know those bridges that you are building? Well, I blow them up," pointing at the pictures on the wall. She chose to distance herself from me from that point and it wasn't too long before they left. After they had left, the lads told me that she so had that coming and that my timing was impeccable.

Let's move back to Dave, our illustrious leader, for the next instalment. We had just arrived in Accra, the capital of Ghana, another beautiful gem on the African coastline. First night in and as usual, all preps were in full swing for that evening's cocktail party. The cocktail party or 'RPC' was particularly successful due in no small part to the local ex-servicemen's association. These were a bunch of old matelots or sailors in their twilight years. Let's not forget that these men supported the World War Two effort by supplying both men and logistics from what was then known as the Gold Coast to Britain and her allies. We were so taken by their humility and their spontaneous humour that we invited them on board the next day for a ship visit. This is something that we do occasionally, particularly when we hit it off with a crowd. We give them what we call the royal tour around the ship and then take them to the mess for drinks and nibbles. We partied all afternoon long, exchanging some lovely stories; it was like listening to your grandad telling his stories. Eventually, and after copious amounts of Courage Special Brew (CSB), we escorted our guests off the ship with an invite and a promise that we would attend their mess the next day, which, of course, we cordially agreed to. The next morning came, and as good as their word, transport arrived in the shape of two mini-buses to take us to the ex-servicemen's mess which was about half an hour away by bus. We would ordinarily take a ship's plaque on these occasions, which, of course, we did, but we also took a barrel of CSB as they had enjoyed it so much the day before.

We were met by their Mess President, a gentleman called Charles. Charles had a wicked sense of humour, much like Dave, which is probably why they got on so well together. We were greeted with hugs and hand-shakes and massive smiles which made us feel very welcome right from the off. After showing us around their facility, we settled down for an afternoon of 'ditting on' which means telling stories and alcohol abuse. What a lovely time we were having. Early in proceedings, Charles stood up and chinked his glass to draw silence, and the mess fell quiet. Charles said some wonderful things about our new-found friendship and toasted 'The Royal Navy'. And so, Dave stood up to reciprocate as is right and proper. He gave a heart-warming speech to our hosts and then proposed a toast; "Gentlemen, please raise your glasses to the honourable men of the Nigerian Navy". The mess fell into silence, an awkward silence, and nothing was said for what seemed like an eternity. Dave had proposed a toast to the Nigerian Navy who are historically enemies of the Ghanaians. Charles looked at Dave and broke the silence by bursting into laugh-ter. By now, he knew Dave and knew that he hadn't proposed the toast with any bad intention; too much alcohol over the last few days had taken its toll. Dave had got confused and whereas you would normally prepare a speech if you were expected to give one, Dave hadn't. Everyone subsequently burst into laughter and we drank the health of the Ghanaian Navy. Not happy with his cock-up and not one to miss an opportunity, Dave stepped up onto the raised podium and started to sing Zulu Warrior. Zulu Warrior is a tribal song from South Africa that sailors usually sing when they are very drunk or prior to stripping naked. We stopped short of stripping off but all joined Dave in the singing and the actions. Charles and his mess loved the Zulu Warrior and I think Dave reinstated our credibility as party people once more. I should probably point out at this stage that Dave's error in geography isn't that bad as Lagos in Nigeria was to be our next port of call. Bless you, Dave; you are a gem. Accra in Ghana was to feature in my life many years later but I will leave that for a later chapter.

Diplomatic Clearance or Dipclear is a process whereby the British Government establishes whether it is safe for a British warship to visit a country. Dipclear does focus on other areas but let's just stick with whether or not it is safe to visit. In all my years in the Navy, this is the only time that I have seen quite obviously that it didn't work. Accompanying the Royal Yacht into Monrovia in Liberia is not the time to be put into an unsafe position, and you might think that if anything, there would be over-the-top checks, rather than very little active intel. As we approached the berthing jetty, we were held off, as the main crane which was to put our gangways in place had fallen over and had gone partially through the jetty which raised the question, how safe is the jetty? Crisis over and one crane later, the Royal Yacht was berthed followed by us. Because of our now very close proximity to the Yacht, we had a big push on cleaning and polishing as there was a cocktail party on board the Yacht later that evening. After the party, some of the guests were invited back to our ship where we entertained them for another hour or two. One of these guests was a local businessman called Eric. Eric was leasing and selling Toyota vehicles to farmers and local industries. Eric invited six of us out the next evening to dinner and drinks; within the navy, we call this process grippoing. Spot on time the next evening, Eric turned up in a stretched limo with a driver to pick us up. He initially took us to a wine-tasting and then on to his club for drinks. After drinks, we were taken to a quaint little fish restaurant for dinner which was lovely. Towards the end of the meal, Eric took a call on the restaurant line to say that his car plant was on fire. He offered to drop us but that was a big detour, so we stayed with him and went to the plant. During our trip to his plant, our car was stopped three times by non-government militia. They were heavily armed with semi and automatic weapons and were quick to point them towards us until they established who we were. Once they were happy, they allowed us to travel on to the next of their impromptu check-points where the same procedure was repeated. Geographically, the restaurant had been right on the outskirts of Monrovia and as we were moving towards the plant, we were also moving towards the coast. As a firearms expert, I can assure you that this experience was particularly uncomfortable, as the guys with the guns looked a little crazy and were definitely not in the mood for wit or comebacks. We behaved ourselves, did as we were told, and arrived at the plant safely. The plant was a raging inferno, with no fire brigade and very little left to salvage. We stayed until about midnight although we were unable to do anything constructive by way of helping. Eric decided to take us back to the ship where we only encountered one of the checkpoints on our journey. Immediately upon our arrival, I spoke to the Duty Officer and strongly suggested he wake the captain and share the news with him. I then turned in for the night. Next morning, all the talk was about the civil unrest and the militia around the outskirts of the city. But strangely, we hadn't sailed. The jetty and adjacent areas were now being patrolled and protected by Royal Marines from on board the Yacht. I don't think they were expecting this sort of role on this trip, but as always, they did a splendid job. As the day went on, we reduced our notice for sea as more and more equipment became available and we sailed early the next day without incident.

I think a little humour might now be in order so I wish to share a story with you about a nun. A year or so after our trip down the West African coast, we found ourselves on another tax-free cruise with grey funnel lines, this time travelling down the Eastern coast of the USA towards the Caribbean. We arrived in Baltimore, Maryland for a four-day stopover and were berthed right in the centre of the city. The city was fantastic and the people of Baltimore were extremely welcoming to us. All the normal diplomatic exchanges were carried out and we got some serious downtime. I, like many, managed to find a lady friend in a club and we became an item for the duration of the visit. There is an unwritten and golden rule as sailors, that if you manage to find a relationship whilst travelling around, it is just a holiday romance and nothing more. The chances are you couldn't see them again even if you wanted to. I was a single man with no commitments but I do know that one or two of the married men chose to mingle with the opposite sex. I'm not condoning their actions but as long as they left it as a holiday romance, no harm would usually come of it. Paddy, our social secretary, found himself a young lady and they really hit it off. We hardly saw Paddy for the duration of our stay there but he was happy enough. He even brought her on board to show her around and to have a drink in the mess. With Christmas fast approaching, Paddy and his lady friend were invited to a fancy-dress party. Paddy dressed as Batman and his lady friend dressed as a nun. Unbeknown to us all, Paddy had shared a secret with his lady friend and that was that he had a thing about nuns. She obliged and dressed up for Paddy wearing her nun's outfit but with stockings, suspenders, and high heels to titillate him. Apparently, fun was had by all and we didn't see Paddy again until we sailed.

During one of my duties whilst alongside, we had just closed the ship to visitors and were settling down to what we hoped would be a quiet evening. As I was the Duty Officer, I spent a lot of my time at the gangway running the ship's routine and overseeing ship security, as well as any necessary ceremonial aspects. It was just beginning to get dark when a limousine pulled up and a gentleman came up the gangway. Behind him, a lad, who turned out to be his son, was getting himself into a wheelchair. The chap asked if they could come on board for a look around as they had missed the opportunity earlier in the day. I pointed out that the ship was open again tomorrow and that they would be most welcome then. He seemed a little disappointed and said that they were unable to visit tomorrow. I asked how able his son was, as warships are full of obstacles and trip hazards. He said that he just needed to rest occasionally and that he would be fine. So, with this in mind, I decided to allow them a private visit and hosted it myself.

We have a royal route that we use when an impromptu tour is needed, which is essentially the upper deck, the operations room, the bridge, and the weapons. During this walkabout, the gentleman, whose name was Tom, was extremely pleasant and very grateful for the tour. I warmed to Tom and so offered him a drink in the mess. He said that he didn't drink alcohol. I assured him that I could find tea, coffee, or soft drinks, and he was chuffed and said yes. Once we entered the mess, one or two of my colleagues thought that they recognised him and when he introduced himself formally, it turned out that he was Tom Clancy, the much-acclaimed author and bestseller. The name Tom Clancy didn't mean anything to me as I wasn't the most literary of scholars; he was just Tom, this nice chap I had met. After a brew, I escorted Tom and his son off the ship and wished them well.

Much to my surprise, the very next morning, Tom's limo turned up and his driver brought up a box for me and apologised that Tom couldn't be here in person as he had a business meeting to attend. I thanked the driver and took the box to the mess to open. Inside the box were about six different books all signed by the author, Tom Clancy, along with Christmas wishes. It was one of each of his books to date; wow! Thinking, rather naively, that these books were all mine, Dave, the President, reminded me that they were effectively a present to the ship and that I should spread them around accordingly. I took, and still have, a copy of 'Red Storm Rising' and then passed on the other books one to each mess and they were to be included in their own respective Christmas raffles.

After what had been a lovely break, we sailed from Baltimore and I noticed that Paddy's young lady was on the jetty to see him off. They discretely waved to each other as we slipped and proceeded to sea, never to see each other again. Well, that last statement isn't exactly true. Making our way towards Tampa in Florida, Paddy told us that he was so taken with his lady friend that they had arranged to meet again in Florida. It would be very easy to go on about how good the stop in Tampa was, particularly as it was Superbowl time and everyone was partying, but I want to pick up on the nun story. Incidentally, the New York Giants beat the Buffalo Bills by twenty to nineteen. Paddy was obviously smitten with his lady friend as they did everything together. He even shared that she had worn the nun's outfit for him on two more occasions. However, nothing lasts forever and once we left Tampa, they would never meet again. Now someone, and I think it was maybe our chippy, had acquired a Barbie doll and dressed her as a nun, stockings and all. This was presented to Paddy as a memento of his time in the States. Paddy's new-found friend spent the next few weeks alongside his bunk reminding him of the good times that he had had.

The deployment was coming to its conclusion and we started to make our way across the Atlantic. Paddy pointed out that he couldn't keep the nun as his wife might find her and then he would have to explain. So, with a heavy heart, he decided to get rid of her. Having a good working relationship with the captain, I spoke to him about the possibility of doing a burial at sea for the nun. He was totally on-side and thought that it was a great idea. So, I got the chippy to make a wooden coffin and a tilting frame. The first Sunday at sea was lovely weather with a becalmed sea, so the scene was set. At nine o clock, the Navigating Officer slowed the ship right down and announced that there would be a short service on the flight deck. Paddy and I had already taken the nun and given it to the chippy to seal in the coffin, and there was even a little cross on the front. On the flight deck, the tilting frame was erected and covered with a union flag. Most of the ship's company mustered on deck to witness this burial at sea. The captain said a few short words and then placed the coffin on the tilting frame and underneath the flag. Paddy himself decided to launch the coffin into the ocean by pulling on the handle and watching the coffin slide out from under the flag and into the water with a splash. This was the end of an era.

Within each mess deck, we carry out secret Santa each year and, as we were at sea this time, it was a nice break from operational commitment. Well, wasn't everybody surprised when Paddy opened his secret Santa and found a Barbie doll dressed as an angel. You could have blown him over with a feather because he realised that it was the same doll but now dressed as an angel. You could see that he was perplexed as he had seen the nun's burial at sea and witnessed her plunging beneath the waves. How could this be? Paddy is usually the prankster and doesn't normally get caught out, so this was sweet revenge. The chippy had placed a bow-shackle in the coffin instead of the doll prior to sealing it, and had hidden the doll away. Now we were laughing at Paddy's expense, poor old soul. The angel spent the rest of the Christmas period on top of our Christmas tree. Once all the festivities were over and the decorations came down, Paddy took the angel to the upper deck and discharged her overboard never to be seen again.

After a lovely break in the UK spending some down-time with families, it was time to deploy again, this time a totally different sort of deployment to the Persian Gulf. We made our way through the Mediterranean and Suez Canal into the Red Sea. Once in the Red Sea, we met HMS Brilliant which was just about to leave the 'Gulf' as we were relieving her. Both ships stopped in the water and staff were exchanged for the operational handover. This was normal procedure as it was good practise from both a practical viewpoint and from a security view-point. My opposite number on board HMS Brilliant was a Scottish chap called Jimmy Green whom I had known for quite some years. Jimmy arrived by helicopter along with other key players and, as I was hosting him, I took him to the office for our briefing/de-briefing. As soon as

I saw Jimmy, I noticed that both of his hands were heavily bandaged. This was my first Gulf patrol and I really didn't know what to expect but what I didn't expect was to get that close to the action. I questioned Jimmy about the injuries to his hands and, rather embarrassingly, he told me that they had had a 'leaving the Gulf' party the night before and among other drinks were flaming sambucas. Part of the ritual of drinking flaming sambucas is that you put your hand over the glass to extinguish the flame before you drink them. Jimmy had tried to do two at a time and failed miserably; neither flame extinguished and spillage onto both hands caught fire and burned him.

Once we arrived in theatre, we quickly adapted to life on active patrol. Four hours on-watch, four hours off-watch, for a month; four meals a day and very little daylight as we stayed in defence watches for the duration. After a very tedious and mainly inactive patrol, we were stood down to Dubai for a restore, refuel, repair, rest, and relaxation. I had decided to take some station leave whilst in Dubai as I had friends living there. Anne Marie and her husband Chris had been living in Dubai for about five years. Ann Marie had moved into the same street as my family back in the UK when we were all much younger so I knew all about her, but nothing about her husband Chris, who ran his own landscaping business. My sister Pepe had visited Ann Marie and Chris twice previously and, once they knew

I would be visiting Dubai, they insisted that I come and stay with them. I was below decks readying myself to be picked up to go to Ann Marie and Chris's house when a main-broadcast pipe was made to tell me that I had a visitor at the gangway. The visitor was this beautiful blonde with long tanned legs driving an open-top red Mustang with white leather interior. Ann Marie had arrived and boy, did the lads notice! This did my ego the world of good. Ann Marie greeted me with a big hug and a kiss, which got a cheer from the lads. She apologised that Chris couldn't be there because he was working. Part of what Chris's company did was security fencing and there was an unprecedented demand for his services due to Saddam's activities and raised security concerns in the Gulf. Because Chris had to work for such long hours, I only really saw him first thing in the morning and at night. Not being one to complain, Ann Marie took me out and about each day sampling all the best that Dubai had to offer. I suppose the highlight of my time spent there was when Chris organised tickets to the Dubai Tennis Stadium for a Tamla Motown night. On the bill on this particular night was the 'Godfather of Soul', James Brown, the original Four Tops, The Temptations, and The Sound of the Supremes. What a fantastic night and what a lovely way to finish off what had been a brilliant stay.

Once I left the ship, I was drafted ashore to H.M.S. Raleigh, a training establishment in Cornwall. As a

Naval marksman and fully qualified shooting coach, I was privileged in 2001 to be asked to coach and conduct Queen's Medal at Bisley in Surrey. I was entrusted with numerous additional duties which included teaching Rules of Engagement (ROE) to Commanding Officers designated, and troops being operationally deployed. In short, I was trying to explain the difference and the legal position between a shooting incident resulting in a well-done and a pat on the back, or resulting in a charge of manslaughter or murder. As I was working for and alongside Royal Marines, I found the job particularly rewarding as it was a total change in direction for me.

My Sergeant Major was a chap called Des O'Brian, who, when I was serving with him, was the most decorated man in the Royal Marines. Des was 'Mister Royal Marine'; he ate, drank, and slept the Corps. He had even coached the Royal Marines' sniper team. I warmed very quickly to him as he was no-nonsense and extremely professional. As I was the Senior Instructor at Raleigh, Des asked if I'd be interested in assisting him to run Bisley. Needless to say, I said yes, and for the next couple of months, I assisted Des with what, at this stage, was mostly administration. I should add at this point that if I wasn't tied up with ROE, then I would probably be on the ranges conducting live firings with both Naval and Marine students. The reason I mention this is because all manner of shooting teams took advantage of the longer ranges at Raleigh, including the Royal

Navy Shooting Team, who, by definition, include the Royal Marines. Whilst each team brought their own qualified coaches, we might, on occasion, offer some invaluable advice to either the coach or the shooter, in order to improve their output. Let us not forget that the top of my identity card says 'Royal Navy' and the top of a Royal Marines identity card says 'Royal Navy', literally, Brothers in Arms. This is a constructive use of resources and, if in some small way it assists the Navy to beat the Army at Bisley, then so be it.

July came around bringing with it Bisley. Logistically, from our point of view, things were fairly straightforward as we only had to transport ourselves and our own equipment. The various teams from all of the Armed Forces, including Commonwealth Forces, brought their own weapons, ammunition, and stores. We based ourselves at the nearby Browning Barracks. Initial and qualifying shoots were conducted throughout the early stages and as the week went on, a point-tallying system established the best shooters to date. As of yet, I hadn't been involved in coaching although I had assisted Des on numerous occasions.

I feel compelled at this point to lay out a little background information. Earlier in the year, my father was diagnosed with terminal cancer and we were about halfway through his new life expectancy. My dad had spent some time serving with the Parachute Regiment back in the 1950s and so, with Des's permission, I had asked for him to be allowed to attend Queen's Medal Day at Bisley. I should also point out for those who don't know, that the Royal Marines and the Parachute Regiment are probably the most fiercely competitive elements of the Armed Forces, with no love lost. My family home was only about forty minutes by car from Bisley and so on Queen's Medal Day, I drove home to pick him up. He had been so looking forward to this day out and, even though his physical health was failing him, he knew exactly what was going on. Dad had dressed accordingly; he had even put a tie on, which was something he rarely did. When we arrived back at Bisley, Des had organised a field chair for Dad and set him up on the side of the range with a great view. Every one of the Naval and Marine contingent came across to shake Dad's hand, which was wonderful; he looked quite taken aback.

The next part of this story involves skulduggery. Whilst I was conducting the finale to the shoot, The Queen's Medal, Des had taken himself over to the Parachute Regiment tent and had spoken to their Sergeant Major. This took a lot of bottle as the two Regiments really don't get on.

Des had also sent one of our staff back to Browning Barracks to raid the NAAFI of anything related to the Parachute Regiment. Shoot now over, and very successful, I made my way back to Dad. While I was chatting with him, Des came over with a few bits, nothing fancy but very poignant; a pen, a coaster, cuff-links, a tie, etcetera, all with the Paras' logo. Then, completely unexpectedly, the Paras' Sergeant Major came across to meet Dad and brought with him about a dozen young members of the regiment. Des introduced them to Dad and then the Sergeant Major said, "Come and meet a hero that jumped on Suez". This completely took me aback as I hadn't mentioned Suez since I first asked Des about bringing Dad some months earlier. One by one, these soldiers queued to meet Dad and shake his hand; what a phenomenal way to complete the day. Dad had tears in his eyes and I think maybe I did too. Incidentally, the coaster took pride of place on Dad's armchair for the rest of his time.

R.I.P. Dad

CHAPTER 10
MALTA

Next on our journey through life, we come to the beautiful island of Malta. Here, there are two stories spread over two decades. The first starts about ten days before our arrival in Malta. As is naval custom, we began advertising onboard for personnel to man for a 'Malta dog night shoot'. This is almost a rite of passage for young and inexperienced ship's company members to provide a service to the island community of Malta.

Firstly, the advertisement goes out on 'daily orders' which is the onboard publication or daily news outlet. Once advertised, anyone interested in taking part passes their names to the petty officer gunner. As there is a need for one officer and twenty lower ranks, the search goes on in the wardroom (officers' mess) as well. With the team now having been selected, they are mustered in the junior ranks' dining room for a briefing. The captain himself gives the brief to emphasise the importance of the Malta dog night shoot. The skipper then explains that parts of the island are over-run with marauding packs of wild dogs that are essentially nocturnal as they come out to hunt and feed in the coolness of the night. By morning, they return to the wetlands where they hide away until the next night. Now that the dogs are encroaching on the towns, there is a very definite need for action. Because Malta has limited abilities and resources, we often offer military support, subject to diplomatic clearance.

Once selected and briefed, training pushes on in earnest. Naval stores are the first venue for the team, to draw the necessary kit and equipment. Full sets of combat clothing, full sets of waterproof clothing, boots, torches, small spades and much more. Having now been kitted out and stowed their gear, they muster at the sickbay for medicals. The ship's male nurse, or Doc as he is known, carries out a full medical on everyone, checking weight, heart rate, blood pressure, sugar levels, and all things needed. Before team members can leave the sickbay, Doc gives them a suppository which is to counter rabies should they be unfortunate enough to be bitten by one of the Malta dogs. They are ushered into the sickbay toilet where they can insert the suppository in private. Once administered, they can leave. One or two team members were fairly slight in their build and so the Doc said that they needed to work on their upper body strength before landing. He went on to say that if they manage to shoot a dog, then they would have to bury it and so they needed upper body strength; this also explained the need for being issued with a short-handled spade. From day one, after the daily physical training finished on the flight deck, the Physical Training Instructor, or PTI, took an additional session for the Malta dog team, concentrating on upper body strength and recovery rate. This was tough training at any time but in the heat and wearing full combat dress and boots and carrying all equipment, the team was working very hard.

Over the next few days, a feeling of elitism spread throughout the team and they became very competitive. This manifested itself when the team conducted live firings with their now-zeroed rifles over the stern of the ship. Rubbish bags were dropped over the side and the navigating officer positioned the ship about six hundred metres from the bags. Shooting began and one or two 'shooting stars' were born. Diet hadn't been ignored in the run-up to our arrival in Malta and the ship's caterer was aware that they needed to load up on calories and carbs, so a second sitting for evening meals was arranged for the last few days for just the Malta dog team, which included the officer eating with his team. Because the team would be disembarking by boat, boat drills were carried out by the chief boatswain's mate. These would include who sits where, who is in first, arcs and areas of responsibility with rifles, and, very importantly, who gets out first to secure the jetty area. So as not to breach any international rules on the legality of the landing and to avoid it constituting an invasion, any ammunition involved would be issued once ashore by the Maltese authorities and the issue and use of the ammunition would be controlled by the officer in charge.

The day before our arrival in Malta, the ship's intelligence officer mustered the entire team, which included key players such as the captain, the navigating officer and the engineer. A thorough brief on the disembarkation was given, followed by an extensive brief on the operating areas. Radio call signs were issued and emergency procedures were covered. Final brief given, time for an early night as it was an early start the next morning.

After an earlier than usual breakfast, the team went to the weapons store and drew weapons. Now fully suited and booted, they were mustered on the boat deck ready to disembark. Over the ship's main broadcast system came the pipe 'Away Malta dog night shoot team'. This was the cue for everyone to take up their place in the boat. Once embarked, the ship slowed right down and the boat was hoisted out to deck-edge level. You could sense the tension; it was palpable, as some were adjusting their helmet straps or tightening their webbing. Then came the order from the captain on the bridge, 'secure the boat, Malta dog night shoot team stand down'. At this point, two hundred sailors made their way out onto the deck from every hatch and door possible with cameras clicking and video rolling, cheering and laughing at twenty-one individuals who had failed to see that this was a spoof.

To coin a modern expression, 'they had been framed'. There was no Malta dog shoot, there are no wetlands in Malta, there are no unruly packs of dogs, and certainly no need for our intervention. Surprise turned to embarrassment and embarrassment turned to laughter as the penny dropped among the team.

What they had been part of is an age-old initiation package that happens on most warships prior to entering Malta. It works for two reasons; those involved are all first-time visitors to Malta and so they know no different, and those who have been before say nothing because the chances are they were caught out the first time they visited. On this particular occasion, photographs of the 'disembarkation' and the story were sent back to dear old Blighty to our monthly publication called 'Navy News', so the Malta dog night shoot team had to relive the embarrassment again with their loved ones once they were home; shame. And finally on this story, if you were worried about the suppository that they took, they were just placebos so no lasting damage was done.

The second of my two Maltese stories happened about twenty years later. Whilst serving as a Chief Petty Officer on board HMS Cumberland, we paid a visit for what would turn out to be my last time whilst serving. As the ship approached Grand Harbour, I noticed that the entrance to the harbour looked different. On top of Fort Saint Angelo was a structure that was new to everyone; it turned out to be part of a set for the filming of 'Gladiator'.

This set was a scale model of Rome's Colosseum and was the backdrop, along with some computer wizardry, for the later scenes in the movie. Okay, excitement over, and after the ship was successfully berthed alongside in Valletta, a crowd of us from the mess decided that as we were quite late in our careers, we would go ashore and re-visit some old stomping grounds.

We headed off for an area known as 'The Gut'. The Gut, now known as Straight Street, was a street lined with terraced properties containing sleazy bars and brothels, tattoo parlours and greasy-spoon eateries, and everything that a sailor might want. Whilst en route to The Gut, we decided that the only way to mark our return to Malta was with a tattoo. When we arrived, imagine our surprise and disappointment at the changes that had taken place. No more brothels and bars of ill-repute, no more tattoo parlours, in fact, nothing that reminded us of what had been there in the past. There was now a lovely tree-lined avenue with boutiques and souvenir shops, well-appointed terraced housing, and some very plush-looking bars and restaurants.

I suppose because Malta has such a large tourist population, it was inevitable that the ancient relics, which were home to so many sailors over past years, would be brought into the twentieth century. Visits to Malta by warship are very few and far between and the demands of tourism by far outweigh the demands of old sea-dogs.

Now, there is never a time when a sailor doesn't know what to do. All he has to do is find a watering hole within which he can discuss a way ahead. We were in Valletta and found a really old-fashioned pub, believe it or not, called 'The Pub'. The landlord made us very welcome and we settled down for a drink or two. The conversation was very much about the old days in Malta and how things had changed. The afternoon went on, and, apart from two or three locals, we had the place to ourselves. The drinks flowed so well that we decided to abandon our efforts to get a tattoo and stay for a drinking session instead. When sailors get serious about drinking, it becomes very competitive and so challenges are thrown out, the winner chooses the next shot, and the loser downs it. This went on for quite some time and by now, we were quite merry. From the entrance to the pub came a voice asking us if we were British. Two men and a woman were stood there in the doorway and once we confirmed that we were indeed British, and from the warship, they asked to join us. It turned out to be the very recognisable actor Oliver Reed and what we took to be his girlfriend and agent. Ollie wanted to buy us all a round of drinks but we said no and bought them a round of drinks. Ollie liked the drinking games that we were playing and got very actively involved. He introduced a few challenges of his own, like bear-hugs and arm-wrestling, each with drinking penalties for winning and for losing. This was developing into a great afternoon of drunkenness and debauchery. At some time during the session, Ollie sat down on one of the benches that surrounded the bar saying he felt ill. Could it be that the party animal himself had met his match…? No, we were woefully wrong. Ollie's lady friend sat with him and cradled his head in her lap as Ollie put his feet up on the bench. After a short while, Ollie's health took a downward turn and the lady friend asked the other gent to call an ambulance. The ambulance arrived within five minutes or so and took Ollie and the lady to hospital. The other gent stayed put. Suddenly, his mobile phone rang and he went ashen. He told us that Ollie had died of heart failure on his way to hospital! Well, for as much as Ollie knew how to party, he also knew how to end one.

Once we took in the magnitude of what had just happened, we did the only thing that we could under these circumstances; we went to a nearby t-shirt shop in The Gut and had t-shirts made up with 'We killed Ollie Reed' on the front with his picture. As we made our way back to the ship, we had to go through a security gate. At the gate was a very attractive young lady who turned out to be a reporter for the Sun newspaper; doesn't news travel fast? She picked up on our t-shirts straight away but before she could ask us anything, our public relations officer swooped in and instructed us to go back to the ship and say nothing. Upon our arrival on board, our First Lieutenant, who is the second in command, told us to remove the t-shirts and that he didn't want to see them again. As I look back over the years, I feel that Ollie got a great send-off, albeit not by intention; he partied hard until his last. God bless you, Ollie Reed, you died as you had lived.

CHAPTER 11
SHORT STORIES

As I delve into the depths of my memory, I begin to recall stories that I had long forgotten. Some of these stories are no more than a short paragraph. I thought I would utilise this chapter for some of those freshly recalled memories. During the early 1970s, we were on patrol and our fresh provisions were beginning to run low as we had been at sea for quite some considerable time. As we weren't due to go into harbour for some two more weeks, the captain and the supply officer came to a decision. A broadcast was made closing up the sonar operators into the sonar control room.

Once closed up, the operators were tasked with trying to find a decent size shoal of fish. After an hour or so, we located a sizable shoal, at which point the captain closed up the mortar crews and had our mortar mark 10, which was lovingly known as Squid, loaded with a high-explosive round. Having checked the safety of the area and setting the appropriate depth, we fired a live mortar into the perceived position of the fish. After witnessing the impressive spectacle of a depth bomb going off, the ship was manoeuvred over the blast area where dead fish were rapidly appearing on the surface. Our sea boat was dispatched to recover the fish and was gone for about an hour. Once the boat returned, we called our laundrymen to the upper deck to help identify the edible fish from the non-edible. We carried two laundrymen onboard, both from Hong Kong, and they were what was known as locally employed personnel or LEP. Being Asian, a large part of their diet was fish, and they catered for themselves, out of choice, in the laundry. So, our two laundrymen set about sorting the fish. Whilst much of the fish was recognisable and edible, some were less so. Some of the 'less so' was taken by them and some of the 'less so' was ditched overboard. After hosing down the boat and the flight deck, we continued with our patrol. Even though it wasn't Friday, there was plenty of fish on the menu for the next few days. Well done the sonar men and the mortar crews.

On one of my many tours in the Atlantic, we were escorting the Royal Yacht and the Royal Standard was flying over her. This indicated that Her Majesty the Queen was resident. On one Saturday afternoon at sea, we received a signal from the Yacht asking for twelve volunteers to attend a church service the next morning on board the Yacht. I am not a religious person but felt that this was an opportunity not to be missed. So, along with the other volunteers, I made sure that my white dress suit was up to standard, polished my medals, and whitened my shoes in readiness for the next day's visit. One of the Royal Barges was dispatched to collect us and took us to Britannia, the Royal Yacht. Once on board, we were met and greeted by one of the Royal Household, who escorted us to the chapel and briefed us on our conduct. We were told to only fill up the rows from row three back as The Queen doesn't like anybody standing immediately behind her. The organist began to play some incidental music whilst we were waiting. Then, and very unexpectantly, Her Majesty appeared from the front of the chapel and not the rear as we had believed. She had with her the two children of the Duke and Duchess of York, namely, Princesses Beatrice and Eugenie, plus a small entourage. The Queen greeted us and smiled. Once settled, the service began. Whilst we were singing one of the hymns, I suddenly realised that I was only about three feet behind the Monarch and I had a tremendous feeling of pride overcome me. I had worn the Queen's Crown on my uniform all these years and here was the actual Queen, although she didn't have a crown on. Another memory that I shall cherish.

The Royal Yacht fully dressed

HM The Queen, HRH Prince Phillip & The Duchess of York
onboard Britannia with HMS Active

During the early 1980s, I was spending long periods of time in defence watches, which is watch on, watch off, for as long as the tactical situation requires it. These watches are tedious and almost detach you from reality, as you are in a dark place seeing no sunlight and monitoring detection equipment for protracted periods of time. When we were relieved on patrol and stood down, we were sent to Genoa in Northern Italy. Observing the date in the sporting diary and identifying an opportunity, my mate John and I sought permission from the captain to go to Monaco for the Monte Carlo Grand Prix Qualifiers. With the captain's permission and a train ticket from Genoa to Monaco, we set off. The journey was to take about three and a half hours by train to cover the 114-mile journey, so it was a very early start. We slept for most of the journey but arrived at about ten in the morning.

This is the qualifiers prior to the race. Gilles Villeneuve can be seen at the front in his Ferrari, followed by Nigel Mansell in his Lotus competing in his first full year in F1. Carlos Reutemann can be seen third in his Saudia Williams. Villeneuve won the 1981 Grand Prix.

After finding probably the most expensive breakfast I have ever had, we made our way to the race circuit. My first impression was just how small the circuit was; you could walk around it in about an hour and a half, and indeed, we did. Once we made our way to the waterfront, we could take in the entire spectacle, and boy, was it impressive. The sessions hadn't started yet so we took in the sights. If you love your cars then this is the place to be, and I don't just mean race cars. I was brought up as a child near Ascot and when there was a race meeting, you would see some of the best cars in the world, but this beat that into a cocked hat. Cooped-up Bentleys, very specialised Porsches, Lamborghinis and Ferraris lined most access points to the race circuit. There was definitely a 'French Riviera' feel about things. John and I found two vantage points to watch the qualifying heats, one at each end of the street circuit. Famous names were racing, like Carlos Reutemann, Nigel Mansell, Nelson Piquet, and Alain Prost. We even saw Mario Andretti crash off the circuit and get craned off, although, after a brief check-up at the hospital, he was fine. Even though the race wasn't until the next day, John and I had the time of our lives; we were like two little schoolboys. All good things must come to an end and in this case, it was an abrupt end. Our ship was sailing on Monday and we had to get back across the border and into Italy, which we duly did.

Whilst providing a security presence within the Mediterranean as part of 'Standing Naval Force Mediterranean', or 'Stanavformed', we found ourselves in the port of Haifa in Israel. This was my first visit to Israel and I intended to get in as much sightseeing as possible. A bus trip was organised from Haifa, via Tel Aviv, to Jerusalem. This was a trip of a lifetime and not to be missed. The bus departed and we made our way along the coast towards Tel Aviv; to be honest, there wasn't much to see at this point; it was 'just another city'. As we cleared Tel Aviv, our hostess told us that we were beginning our ascent to the Holy Land. This was a 45-mile journey, all of which was uphill, as Jerusalem was some 3,800 feet above both Tel Aviv and sea level. We were told in no uncertain terms to prepare ourselves both spiritually and physically for the uphill journey.

Progress was painfully slow, but, unlike in Tel Aviv, there were more things of interest to see. The scenery was dry and arid. Whilst arid would seemingly imply nothing, there were remnants of the 'War of Independence' in the form of discarded and wrecked military equipment which has been intentionally left as monuments to the battle to control the Jerusalem Corridor. After maybe thirty miles or so, the hostess announced that we would be stopping shortly for a refreshment break and to get fuel. Bear in mind that we are now very hyped up about the 'Promised Land' with its rich history. We are close to the holy city of three major religions; Islam, Christianity, and Judaism. What we saw next was totally unexpected and caught everyone off balance. We pulled into an American-type diner and complex. This was no ordinary diner; it was, and I believe still is, the largest collection of Elvis Presley memorabilia in the world outside of Nashville. Strange, surreal, odd, and unexpected are expressions that spring to mind. Outside the diner was a huge statue of Elvis and you walked underneath a subway, which was fully adorned with Elvis memorabilia, into the main diner, again fully adorned. After a very pleasant break and the coach re-fuelling, we continued our journey for the remaining fifteen miles or so. Once in the promised land, I did everything that time would allow. Nazareth, Bethlehem, Sea of Galilee, the Wailing Wall, Garden of Gethsemane, and more. I collected souvenirs, I took photographs and I soaked up the beauty that surrounds this area. However, my lasting impression of this trip was having been told to prepare spiritually and then coming across the Elvis story. Funny world?

Elvis lives?

The author and Elvis but which is which?

This is the actual birthplace of Christianity

The author at the Wailing Wall

Dome of the Rock and the Wailing Wall

This time, the decade is the early 1990s and the location is St. Thomas in the US Virgin Islands. Having spent the day at the beach, I was on board having just had my supper, when I decided to take my mug of tea onto the upper deck to soak up the night lights of St. Thomas. Whilst I was on the forecastle, James, my mate, joined me. James was on duty and so was in full uniform. We were small-talking, or 'ditting on' as we call it in the navy, when James noticed shadows moving in the rocks underneath the ship's bow. Scouring the areas under the ship, we saw the shadow of a person with a rifle. Suddenly and without notice, we had a very real situation developing right under our noses. I told James to go and raise the alarm whilst I observed the movements of the rifleman. Within a moment or so of James leaving me, the ship's main broadcast alarms went off and the response force was activated.

I think I should point out at this juncture that the Royal Navy had only armed its sentries barely two years earlier. This was to be the first time that any British warship had responded to a potential armed attack utilizing the newly formed 'Ship's Protection Organisation'. When a ship is alongside and the security state dictates, three operational sentries are deployed as a matter of course; they are the Quartermaster, who runs the ship's routine, and the Bosun's Mate, who assists the Quartermaster, both of whom man the main gangway. The third sentry is the Upper Deck Sentry, who roams around the upper deck. All three sentries are armed with weapons that are loaded with live ammunition. Ordinarily, these three armed sentries can cope with most scenarios but should they need support there is a response force. The response force is taken from the duty watch on a daily basis and are fully briefed first thing every morning by the duty officer. They have pre-designated positions on the upper deck to go to, in order to afford the ship 360-degrees protection. They also have loaded weapons locked away and their own copy of the rules of engagement so that they can respond more quickly.

When the alarm is raised over the broadcast, nothing is said that might warn anyone within earshot as to what is going on. Part of the quartermaster's job is to contact local emergency services and brief them. The singularly most important piece of information that has to be passed is that we have operational sentries deployed on deck with assault rifles and live ammunition. This is to hopefully reduce any chance of blue on blue, or friend on friend firearm exchanges. Our team is subsequently briefed on what sort of response they can expect to see on the jetty for the same reasons. After only a few short moments of waiting, the St. Thomas police service had about six vehicles arrive at the jetty area with sirens blaring. They were mostly American officers and I made my way down to meet and brief them. For the record, we were on the disengaged side of the ship where we couldn't be seen from the area where we had seen the rifleman. Once we had passed security of the jetty over to them, they began using vehicle-mounted spotlights to search the rocks under and around the ship. In next to no time, the police located a man with a rifle who was making his way up from the rocks. They initially apprehended him and took his rifle, which turned out to be an air rifle. After questioning the gentleman, the situation was quickly resolved. The gentleman was 'ratting', or killing rats. He had come up from the area of the rocks because of all the activity on the jetty. Oblivious to the commotion he had caused, the gentleman was warned off by the police for ratting so close to a warship and was told that he shouldn't come ratting in that area again. I thanked the police on behalf of the ship and wished them well. Our response force was de-briefed and then stood down. I went over to the gentleman who had caused all the fuss and asked him a few questions. One of the questions was, "Does this ratting happen regularly?" He assured me it did, then went on to say that any of the superyachts that carry firearms do this to practise their shooting. I queried why they needed to practise shooting. As it was getting quite late, the gentleman, whose name was Dean, said, "Why don't you come around for coffee tomorrow morning and I'll explain in more detail?" We wished each other goodnight, shook hands, and parted.

The author and the heavily armed yacht

The next day at the appointed time, James, who had now finished his duty, and myself, arrived at the yacht that Dean lived on. This was a gin palace on a huge scale. The yacht itself, we found out, cost eighteen million dollars, and Dean, along with six other crew members, looked after the yacht in the absence of the owner, who only used it occasionally. Dean served us up a lovely cappuccino before taking us to an area on the port side which is where coats and jackets can be hung. Dean stopped where we were and turned to us and said that the reason boats' crews need to keep up their target practice is that, "Here in the Caribbean, piracy is rife." Most of the superyachts now carried firearms, and, although the legal side of this is a little vague, the crews are expected to defend their own yacht should it become necessary. Dean then turned one of the coat hooks and pulled out a sliding panel that you would never have guessed was there. Mounted within this wall panel were four assault rifles, four machine pistols, two semi-automatic machine guns, six pistols, and a box of hand grenades plus three air rifles. There was also a stowage full of ammunition. I said to Dean jokingly, "You've got more firepower than I could have put out on deck last night!" We laughed, and then, after another cappuccino and a tour of this beautiful yacht, we said our goodbyes and went our separate ways.

My next memory is one of meeting some genuine but little-known heroes. Before I can discuss them, I need to lay down a little background. During World War 2, there was a battle that would go down in the annals of history. Five Victoria Crosses and eighty other bravery medals were awarded for involvement in the 'Raid on St. Nazaire'. For those unaware of the story, I will precis 'The Raid on St. Nazaire', also known as 'Operation Chariot'.

Whilst the German battleships Bismarck and Tirpitz were wreaking havoc on allied shipping, the 'Department of War' realised that the only dock on the Atlantic seaport capable of supporting either of these two capital warships was St Nazaire on the river Loire, in German-occupied France. As there were far too few British warships available to use, an American destroyer, USS Buchanan, was leased and re-commissioned as HMS *Campbeltown*. The plan itself was fairly simple. *Campbeltown* would have all excess equipment and fittings removed in order to reduce her weight. She had her hull and forward superstructure armour-plated and three tons of high explosive was concreted into her bow. Because of the depth of water in the Loire, the only realistic chance of getting her to her target was to go in on a spring tide, so the date was set for 28th March 1942. Eighteen other smaller boats were involved carrying mostly Commandos and their explosive equipment plus a Motor Torpedo Boat for protection from the rear.

Having sailed from Falmouth, the small flotilla made its way to the entrance of the Loire without incident. They travelled along the Loire under the cover of darkness and flying German flags until they were about a mile or so from the target. At this point, they were challenged by a gun position and were ultimately engaged by it. *Campbeltown*, very cleverly, called up one of the other ships in the flotilla and asked why they were being fired upon by friendly units. This act of deception bought them a little more time, until, within sight of the dock and facilities, *Campbeltown* struck her German flag and raised the White Ensign. All hell let loose! The Germans could now see what they were dealing with and brought down an unparalleled amount of firepower onto the flotilla. *Campbeltown* increased speed to her maximum of 19 knots and headed straight towards the dock. Many of the ships and boats within the flotilla were being severely damaged or sunk as they tried to progress. Campbeltown struck the main dock almost exactly on time. The impact of her hitting the dock lifted her 10 metres or 33 feet up and onto the dock but she didn't explode. Commandos went running ashore to engage the enemy. The ancillary units went to their respective targets with their explosives and began to destroy tugs, winch-rooms, generators, and some of the smaller docks. After a massive fire-fight, more than two hundred sailors and soldiers had been killed or taken as prisoners of war. As the fighting ceased, the Germans believed that the mission had failed because everything was ultimately repairable in a few short weeks. In the aftermath of the battle, the Germans began to go on board Campbeltown to view the damage and see what needed to be done in order to get the dock back in use. Campbeltown's delayed charges suddenly went off, killing 360 German Officers in the process. This wasn't a failed mission but an unparalleled success; the dock was destroyed and was out of action for what would be five years.

Whilst serving onboard the current HMS Campbeltown in the mid-1990s, we were on a routine visit to Brest, in France. We had been told to expect some veterans from 'Operation Chariot', who were known as 'Charioteers'. Our brief was simple; show them around the ship, make them feel welcome, and feed and water

163

them as required. *The Warrant Officers' and Chief Petty Officers' Mess hosted the visit and it was our honour to do so. About a dozen or so of these eighty-plus-year-old gentlemen made their way on board and we hosted them as real heroes. The first thing that hit me about these chaps was their humour, and secondly, their recall and memory. After the ship's tour, we took them for nibbles in the mess and then we hit the bar, as always; the Courage Special Brew, or CSB, was the chosen tipple. We had been listening to their many stories of the war when another guest joined us; she was a journalist from a French Military magazine. With her, she carried a copy of the magazine that she worked for, which had published a special cover story covering the fiftieth anniversary of the 'Raid on St. Nazaire'.*

The photographs that were in this magazine had been taken by a war photographer and pulled no punches. These were the actual photos taken on the night of the raid; wow! What followed was almost surreal. The chaps were sitting around and looking at these pictures and were reminded of things they hadn't seen since 28th March 1942. Suddenly, Mike, one of the guests, said, "Look, Jock, that's you just before you were shot". Jock looked at the picture and said, "Yeah, but they didn't keep me for very long, did they?" Apparently, Jock was known as a tunnel rat because he was always escaping German stalags or prisons. Once he recovered from his bullet wound, he decided it was time for him to leave but he realised that the stalag was a tough place to escape from, so he climbed a ten-foot wall and crossed over into the prison hospital that was adjoined. Breaking his leg as he fell down the other side of the wall and bleeding quite badly, he went straight to a doctors' dressing room and grabbed a white coat and a stethoscope. Then, as bold as brass, Jock just walked out of the prison hospital as if he was a doctor. He was passing guards and dog patrols without incident until one of the German Shepherd dogs picked up on the blood now showing quite clearly on his tunic. The dog handler questioned him in German but he didn't speak a word of it; he was rumbled.

Then Fred, one of the Commandos, pointed out a picture of someone they called 'Daisy'. Fred choked up before he could continue with the story. Once Fred was able to, he told the story of Daisy. Very early in the assault on the dock, Daisy had been blown into the water by an explosion. Daisy had been on one of the Fast Patrol Boats that was trying to get to the winch-house. The river was now ablaze with spilled fuel from damaged and sinking ships and gunfire all around. As Campbeltown passed closely by Daisy in the water, he reached up for someone to grab him. Fred told him, "We can't stop now, mate, we'll pick you up on the way back". Fred was one of only a handful of people that knew this was now a one-way trip and that Daisy was left on his own, never to be seen again. This story had stayed with Fred all of his life and he remembered it in intricate detail. There were many other stories taken from these old veterans as they were working their way through the photographs in the magazine, as if the pictures were reminding them of actions taken on that night of bravery. I take off my hat to you gentlemen; you are indeed true heroes.

HMS Campbeltown, one of my later ships, carries the battle honours for St. Nazaire. Incidentally, she is the only ship in the Royal Navy showing a blue circle with a white star around her crest; this is to signify her relationship with the American navy, specifically USS Buchanan

Something a little closer to home now. A good friend of mine called Gwilym introduced me to the game of rugby union in the most bizarre of ways. It was quite late in my career and I was certainly too old to be playing rugby, so Gwilym arranged for us to go to the annual rugby match between 'The Army' and 'The Navy' at Twickenham, the home of English rugby. Gwilym, an ex-player himself, had moved away from playing regularly, and turned to supporting and spectating more, as, like me, he was well into his career. The stadium is in London's Richmond, on the River Thames, and is played at the end of April or the beginning of May. I actually attended this spectacle twice during my career but I am going to concentrate on my first visit.

At a ridiculously early hour on the day of the game, we all mustered in the Warrant Officers' and Chief Petty Officers' Mess for breakfast. I was serving at HMS Dryad just outside of Portsmouth with Gwilym. Breakfast was simple and efficient; bacon baps, Bucks Fizz, and coffee. After a very basic but delicious breakfast, we were invited to board our respective coaches. Once full, the coaches began to depart. As soon as the coaches were on the road, or even sooner, the beer was broken out. All of the overhead stowage had been filled with cases of lager, cider, and beer. For a while, you had a choice of what you drank, but when there was no choice, you had what you were given. Now, I am more a social drinker than a serious drinker and I couldn't think of anything worse than starting to drink alcohol at this unearthly hour, but after the first two or three, they became quite palatable and went down with much more ease. The drinking would continue throughout our journey with just a short stop for a toilet break, although by now, there were numerous partly 're-filled' cans sitting around. As there was very little mixed company on the coaches, there were no embarrassing 'reveals', as the ladies' Army versus Navy rugby wouldn't take off until the 2020s.

On our arrival at Twickenham, the coaches pulled into their parking places as opposed to backing in. This was because they all had stores at the back of the coach that needed unloading. Usually, two collapsible tables and a chair or two were set up before filling the tables with booze and food. Unbeknown to me, the caterers had been busy the night before preparing lunch on a grand scale, and we carried as much booze as the coach had room for. This was obviously a tried and trusted routine as every coach that pulled in seemed to go through the same process.

Next came the 'walkabout'. Once your coach was set up and settled, you went for a walk around the many other coaches, both navy and army. Everyone hosted everyone else and I can't think of a more convivial atmosphere. You might bump into friends that you hadn't seen in years, or you may bump into people that you met last time out and were just renewing friendships. Amazingly though, with all this booze flowing and all the testosterone in evidence, there was no trouble and I am assured there never is, just banter; how refreshing. Almost all of the coaches take no money for food or drink from the back, but most have a charity box with donations going to their chosen charity. You eat and drink where you want to, mixing with whoever you wish.

Suddenly, and without too much notice, we are summoned into the ground for the game. Making our now drunken way to our seats, we settled down for the match. During the 1970s, the Navy were the dominant force on the field. During the 1990s, the Army were to become the dominant force. Here, we were mid-way through the 1980s watching two sides that were pretty evenly matched. Only the lower tier at Twickenham is open for this fixture as the attendance numbers dictate that this is all that is needed. All Army supporters and all Navy supporters are pretty much together and yet there was no trouble, and rarely is. What limited police presence is required tends to stay out of sight as it infrequently, if ever, kicks off. Everyone continues to drink and there is almost a carnival-like atmosphere.

By now, we had been drinking for about eight or nine hours and even though we don't remember the result of the game, we do remember that we had had a great day so far. When we returned to our coaches, we embarked and set off for our respective home bases. Some sleeping was done on the return journey but most continued drinking, albeit at a slightly more moderate pace. Again, we had the obligatory toilet stop in the middle of nowhere before a late evening arrival back at HMS Dryad. Now you would think that this would be the end of the day, but no, not at all.

An evening do had been arranged in the mess and was due to start shortly, so it was back to your cabin, shower, get into uniform, and then back to the bar. Only the bold were still standing unaided, but I'm proud to say that I hadn't let Gwilym down yet. The social got going and for the next couple of hours, it was music, dancing, and yet more drinking. At some time during the night, Gwilym said that he was hungry. So, on the edge of the camp, there was a little caravan that sells the 'best burgers ever', amongst other things. This place was called 'Dot's' and she always looked after the lads when they were hungry, or drunk, or both. We ordered food and ate it there. I think we may actually have ordered more food whilst we were there and ate that as well. Now suitably replenished, we began to make our way back to the mess. Gwilym desperately needed a pee so he found a bush and did as nature required. I walked on a few steps and then stopped to wait for him. When I looked around, Gwilym was gone! I called out to him but initially, there was no reply. After a while, Gwilym responded to my calling him, although I still couldn't see where he was. I walked back looking for him and there, lying in the tall daffodils, was Gwilym doing his best impression of a snow angel. He'd gone all soft and soppy on me, so I knew it was time to get him home to his bed.

My next short story is centred in 1970s Portsmouth in Hampshire. As a young Leading Rate, I was drafted to Fraser Gunnery Range in Eastney, near Portsmouth. Fraser Gunnery range, or FGR as it was known, was where all live firings for the larger guns, were conducted for the South East of England. Although FGR was administered by HMS Excellent, it was very much a stand-alone unit. As I look back at my time there, there are two stories that I recall. One involves a dog called Rupert. Rupert came to FGR as a stray puppy and the watchkeepers took him under their wing by feeding and watering him and giving him shelter. Rupert only ate what we ate and he grew to a ripe old age. The officer in charge had a civil servant as his PA or secretary and, in due course, she was replaced by a new one who had trouble accepting that Rupert was being properly catered for, so she went out and bought a collar and lead, a bowl and a load of dog food. Rupert never left the camp, so why he needed a collar and lead nobody knows. He refused to wear the collar, and, on the one occasion it was put on him, he removed it. As far as the dog food went, he wouldn't touch it, so he continued to eat with us in our dining room. One of our daily chores at FGR was to carry out security rounds at night. To help us with these rounds, a pushbike was made available. It was an old-fashioned Post-Office bike with a big basket carrier on the front. About two hours after sunset, the quartermaster, of which I was one, would set off to check the security of the site and Rupert would come along to keep us company. Rupert would only stay with you if you didn't go too fast. If you did, he would walk back to the office leaving you on your own. Now, Rupert would go everywhere with you on your rounds with one exception; he wouldn't go to the lower camp. He would wait for you to go there, and then, on your return, he would re-join you. This behaviour seemed a little odd but never changed in all the years I used FGR. The main theory for him not going to the lower camp, which is possibly a bit of an old wives' tale, is that FGR allegedly housed Italian prisoners of war during World War 2. The story goes that some of the prisoners died in the lower camp and were buried there. Whether this is the reason and Rupert had a second sense, or it was for some other reason, Rupert never once went to the lower camp. Rupert died some years later and he is buried on the quarterdeck right by where he lived. The second item I would like to share with you, embarrassingly, caught a few people out. When we fire large guns out to sea, as we were doing at FGR, we make tremendous efforts to keep things as safe as we are able. We are legally and duty-bound to ensure all firings are carried out as safely as possible. Part of our procedure is once we have identified our target, we bring our directors to bear. A director is just another name for an optical sight, so, once the sight is pointing safely at the target, we can put a loaded gun on the end of the system. The directors, or optical sights, are mounted very prominently up on the roofs of the buildings in order for them to get the best view for safety. On two occasions in my personal experience, and very many more at other times, there were unacceptable delays in getting the sights to bear and pass their safety reports. Initially, we had no idea why this should be until, on one occasion, the gunnery officer left his station and went to try to find out what was going on.

Just along from FGR was a nudist beach and on this particular occasion, a voluptuous lady was baring all not fifty yards from the directors or sights. Every single sight was trained to its left and the operators were viewing what was on display. Temporarily, firings were stopped, the gunnery officer redirected all concerned and the practice seemed to die off. I wonder on how many occasions a sight operator has said that the range was clear when he was looking at something else!

CHAPTER 12
LIFE AS AN UNDERTAKER

This particular chapter on my journey along 'the dash' is set after a change in career and a change of mind. I left the Royal Navy in January 2007 having spent the previous two years or so working and training towards a life on the cruise liners as a security officer. I was rewarded for all my hard work by being offered a medium-size cruise liner on a world cruise and, unusually, as 'the' Ship's Security Officer, and not the number two, which is the norm. I was by now divorced and missing my little girl, so, with my new girlfriend, who had been my barber for some recent years, we took my daughter out for pizza, her favourite. I proceeded to tell her about my imminent departure to San Diego in Chile, where I would be joining my first merchant ship as a First Officer. Boy, did I miss the brief! My daughter, now about twelve years old, burst into tears and flew off the handle. She told me that I had promised her that when I left the Navy, I would stop going away and spend more time with her; she was right, I had. Once she returned to the table, having gone to the ladies' room to clean herself up, she made it abundantly clear that she wasn't happy with my going away. Her response came back to haunt me many times over. I said to her that I still had bills to pay, mortgage, etcetera, otherwise, I would end up stacking shelves at B and Q. She responded by saying, "What's wrong with stacking shelves at B and Q? At least then I would be able to see you". She was absolutely right and I hadn't gauged the response that I got from her; I had no defence for what she was saying. I spent the next two weeks splitting my time between trying to placate my daughter and trying to get my domestics in place for the trip ahead. She still wasn't happy but more understanding by now.

Some two weeks later, I flew via Paris to San Diego to join my ship. This appointment was very lucrative with an excellent salary, a hospitality allowance and my own cabin suite with maid. But something was missing. For the first time that I could recall, the money was not the most important thing going on here. I had always liked owning nice things and felt that I had earned them, but suddenly, the mercenary approach didn't sit right. I was missing my daughter and girlfriend much more than I had realised I would.

The change of career was something that needed to happen as my time in the Navy was over, but the change of mind was something that I was able to influence, and so, at a very early stage in my life as a First Officer with the Merchant Navy, I spoke to my captain, who was extremely understanding, and he allowed me to fly home from Easter Island in the South Pacific, terminating my contract in the process. Once home, I was able to re-kindle my relationship with my daughter and build up my relationship with my partner who was soon to become my wife. After kicking my heels for a short while and attending no end of job fairs, an offer of work fell into my lap. A colleague from the Navy told me that a local company of undertakers was looking for staff and that our background was exactly what they were looking for. I applied, was interviewed, and was offered the position, all in short succession.

One of the stories that I would like to share with you since becoming an undertaker is one of extreme coincidence spread over a vast area of both distance and time. In one of the earlier chapters of my book, I make references to carrying out Royal Guardship duties with the Royal Yacht Britannia, when we escorted Prince Charles and his bride Princess Diana on their cruise down the west coast of Africa. During this trip back in 1990, we were in Accra, the capital of Ghana, for a routine visit. Part of what we do is diplomatic work on behalf of the British Government.

On this occasion, our liaison officer, whilst working with local authorities, had determined that the main school in Accra needed some help with maintenance logistics and storage issues. He discovered, for example, that their generator hadn't worked for a while and power cuts were common. Our engineers fabricated the spare parts that were needed and fixed the generator, in fact improving its output. Other jobs slightly less grand were re-wiring at various places throughout the school and fixing water leaks with re-plumbing where necessary. Paint brushes were all the rage for those with less technical skills, which is where I placed myself, and the brief was simple; if it stands still, then paint it! Repaired, re-wired, re-plumbed, re-painted, and re-furbished, we completed everything, including making a massive donation of stationery from our naval stores to the school, in about five days. The stationery went down particularly well as they had very little stock for the students. Once completed, there was a massive sense of achievement and pride. The teachers turned out with some of the students to thank us for all the work that we had done. The reason I am telling this story is that Accra in Ghana is about five thousand miles or so from the UK and sits about five hundred miles north of the equator. One of the teachers in the school was a young man called Clayton, who was also an elder in his village, some four hundred miles into the bush. He commuted regularly to school, such was his love for the job.

Fourteen years later, I was working as an undertaker in the local area in the UK and my director told me that we were going to have an African gentleman in full national dress leading the cortege. This was something different and we were really looking forward to the procession. I mustered my hearse and my team at the appropriate departure point, at the appropriate time, and out came this black gentleman in full national dress, with a drum and, believe it or not, a multi-coloured umbrella. This gentleman danced his way along the road with my hearse staying close behind him to protect him from the traffic. He led us all the way to the church where the main service took place. I had a chance to speak to him very briefly outside the church and it seemed he was actively involved with the local African community. After the service, the big talking point was the African gentleman leading the cortege and how infectiously happy he had been, smiling and dancing all the way to the church.

A year or so later, my now wife's friend Linda introduced her new partner, Clayton. My wife warmed to him and invited them both to our home for coffee. They were a very nice couple and conversation was very easy. I told Clayton that I had been to Accra some years earlier and told him about the work we had done. I was gob-smacked to find out that he remembered everything and in so much detail. He was the young teacher whom we spoke about earlier. This was the start of a great friendship, although there were still one or two turns yet. Linda and Clayton went through a difficult stage in their relationship, and sadly, went their separate ways. Whilst Linda chose to have no further contact with us, Clayton did, and we supported him as best we were able. During one of many conversations, usually over an overly expensive cup of coffee, I told him about the African funeral that we had been part of and, you guessed it, he was the chap at the front. What are the chances?

After these massive coincidences, we became, and still are, the best of friends. During the early part of 2020, he married his new girlfriend Carol and we had the honour of being invited to the service and the knees-up afterwards. What a small world.

I'd like to share with you a few short stories centred on a world that is supposedly filled with taboo and closely guarded secrets. I wish to put a disclaimer in at this early stage by saying that I have never been involved in any action that might be conscribed as being disrespectful or insensitive towards either bereaved families or deceased persons. I have my own code of ethics which I stand by, but I do understand, and get involved in, what is commonly known as 'black humour.'

During my many years of employment with the Ministry of Defence, there was little or no mental health support until towards the very end of my career. You occasionally got involved in activities or saw things that were particularly unsavoury and the only way to move beyond these issues was to make light of them, or even laugh at them. Transferring this coping mechanism to the world of the undertaker I found to be a natural step. As was the case during my military career, there was little or no mental health support in the funeral business, although this improved with time. You see, and get involved with, some particularly nasty issues, especially when you are working at night and on-call. I am not going to dwell on specific cases, but, for example, dealing with an elderly individual who has passed is one thing, but dealing with a child is totally different.

Directly involved in the aftermath of suicide, particularly with young people, is something else that haunts you. And it's not just the graphics of the scene that can take its toll on you; how the bereaved family reacts can be quite telling. There may be anger, there may be grief, there may be silence, or they may be at the point of no hope themselves. Throughout the entire gamut of emotions, you need to remain calm, empathetic, and professional. Yes, in its place, and at the right time, 'black humour' is very necessary for releasing emotional pressure, and an integral part of the job.

When I first started in the profession, I was placed on the ambulance under the competent supervision of Jack. Jack was old-school, he knew his stuff, and he was very professional and empathetic. One thing he did that I really liked was that he would talk to them as if they were still alive. So, for example, if he had to sit somebody up to dress them, he might say, "Come on, Agnes, let's get this cardigan on you, and then we can make you comfortable again". His behaviour was very warm and quite endearing. On my second day in the role, we had to go to one of our funeral homes to prepare a lady for her coffin. Jack asked me to lift her legs up whilst he went about cleaning her properly. As I lifted her legs, there was this terrible smell, something I hadn't witnessed before. The smell was a mixture of faeces, urine, lower body smells, body odour and early decomposition. I was about to ask Jack if they always smelled this way when the two directors, who were in the mortuary with us, left because of the smell. Jack assured me that this was a little unusual but he took it in his stride. I had just been involved in my first body preparation.

Let us lighten the mood. Any new recruit to the business goes through whatever the local initiation procedures might be; in our case, we focus on ghosts and hauntings. We had a lady called Alice who ran our mortuary. She raised any paperwork necessary to have deceased persons released from the local hospital morgue and then we transported them to our hub by ambulance. On one particular day, we removed our deceased from two ambulances and stretchered them into our prepping area. We told Alice that there was still one deceased person in the ambulance who was unaccounted for. I climbed into a body bag and lay on the stretcher, then the lads loaded me back onto the ambulance and we waited for the inevitable. Alice came out scratching her head. She removed the stretcher that

I was lying still on and when I felt the stretcher wheels lock, I sat up inside the body bag and groaned. Alice screamed and ran off, poor thing; she even managed to wet herself in the process.

There was another time when one of our new staff members, called Oscar, was being shown around all of our funeral homes to meet the staff, etcetera, by Sam. Sam was one of our directors but he was a joker and a trickster. Sam rang me a few minutes ahead of his tour of the funeral home that I was at and he told me to hide in the ashes archive section which is deep in the belly of the building. This building is really quite old and a little damp and not very well lit in the archive area. I secreted myself behind large double velvet curtains with my back to the storage and waited. Sam arrived with Oscar a few minutes later and I could hear him warning Oscar that parts of this building were supposedly haunted and that if he didn't want to go any further, that was fine. Oscar had no issue with proceeding as he said he needed to see all aspects of the funeral home. As Oscar stepped up to the curtains in this dimly lit and damp-smelling room, I stepped out from the darkness and howled like a banshee. Poor old Oscar, I think we took a few years off his young life! We caught up with him outside the building; he was literally as white as a ghost.

Very early in my tenureship, I was assigned to a funeral that was a little unusual. The deceased and coffin weighed in excess of forty-five stone. This is far too much weight to manually handle and so a mobile crane was used to lower the coffin into the grave whilst the family were kept in an adjacent area. Eight of us were around the grave to assist where possible. Once in the ground, the family and priest made their way towards the grave. We all bowed together as a mark of respect but as we did so, one of my colleagues, forgetting that his mobile phone was in his breast pocket, manage to deposit the phone straight into the grave. Big oops! At this point, there was absolutely nothing he could do other than pray that it didn't go off. Can you imagine as the family arrives at the graveside, a phone rings from within the grave? The devil inside you says ring his phone, but, of course, you don't. Thankfully, the service went without further incident and once the family had left the graveyard, one of the gravediggers retrieved his phone for him.

Once I had settled into the job, the big boss asked if I would mind getting involved with the ceremonial training aspects as I had much experience in this area. I, of course, agreed and set up a localised training regime. At the risk of tarnishing my reputation, I wish to share another story. As part of my duties, I was tasked with training all new staff on various aspects of ceremonial duties and on the proper use of both fleet and ceremonial vehicles. With this in mind, it is a little embarrassing to admit that I was the first hearse driver in our sector to be given a speeding ticket in a hearse. In my defence,

I was only doing 37mph in a 30mph zone. I was rushing to meet an impossible deadline, my next funeral, which, as usual, the planners had failed to give us enough time for, but most importantly, I wasn't carrying a coffin on board. Either way, this episode cost me £80 and a driving awareness course.

Another tale collected along life's journey concerns a removal that my on-call partner Dale and myself did a few years ago. We were called to a local house in the wee small hours where a gentleman had passed. We carried out our duties in our normal and professional fashion on a gentleman that I can only describe as large. I don't mean large as in fat, I mean this guy looked like he had just finished tossing the caber, beard and all, in the highland games, and we were about to leave the premises when the wife of the deceased asked us the strangest of questions. She asked if she could take his eye! The first thing Dale asked was, "Is it a false eye?" After assuring us that it was, she said that she wished to keep the eye in order to make a pendant from it. We naturally complied with her wishes and removed his false eye for her to keep. Whilst we are talking about my on-call, I have two other tragic cases that I would like to mention.

The first was a road traffic incident that happened up-country. A woman was driving her car on the motorway when she crashed into the back of one of those roadworks lorries that has the big arrow on it, instructing you to go around it. She hit the lorry at speed and killed herself and her two children who were in the vehicle with her. The police report says that she fell asleep at the wheel. After the post-mortem, they were repatriated to us for their funeral. The woman's husband and father of the two children asked if they might be placed in a single coffin for the service. This would not normally be acceptable but the local coroner allowed this to happen, so we ordered an outsize coffin especially. When I went into the funeral home on the day of the funeral, the sight that I was greeted with was both beautiful and tragic in equal measures. The mother was laid out with her toddler holding her hand and her baby was in her other arm. That's a memory that you don't forget easily.

My second story is again whilst Dale and I were on call. I had just taken a call from the police to state that there had been a road traffic incident and that two young girls had died at the scene. The location of this call-out was about an hour's drive from where we were based, so I explained this to the police officer. I was just finishing my paperwork and readying myself to go and pick up Dale when another call came in. This time, it was a shotgun suicide and, coincidentally, only about two miles from the other call-out. So, once more, I completed the paperwork and then went off to pick up Dale. When I arrived at Dale's house, believe it or not, I got a third call-out, and, even more strangely, it was within five miles of the other two.

We realised this was going to be a busy night and so went about prioritising our workload. Our logic was to go to the road traffic incident first so that the road could be re-opened. I contacted the police control officer to let him know how long his officers would be waiting for us, but surprisingly, he told me to go to the third one first, which was an old lady at a farm. I questioned his priorities and he explained. When the road traffic incident was called in, there was no knowledge of how many fatalities there were, so two ambulances were dispatched. The duty officer had authorised one of the ambulances to carry the two girls back to the hospital morgue. Knowing we were going to be about an hour or so, the control officer moved the policemen who were on-site, plus the ambulance, to the scene of the suicide and again, the gentleman was taken by the second ambulance to the morgue. We went straight to the farmhouse. When we arrived, I knocked on the door, identified myself, and offered my condolences. I was escorted into a very large reception room where there were about forty or so people. I asked if somebody could show me to where the deceased was and there was a little titter of laughter around the room. The chap showing me around pointed to the chair next to where I was standing and said, "There she is". She had died sitting up on a dining room chair with her eyes open and one arm across the back of the chair. I felt a little silly but no permanent damage.

A little namedropping now perhaps. One of our best-loved TV actresses, Dawn French, lost her mother back in 2012 and we were honoured to be asked to conduct the funeral. Her ex-husband Lennie Henry was there as was her close friend Jennifer Saunders and her husband, Ade Edmondson. As I was first at the funeral, part of my job was to place orders of service around the chapel. I had already been told that there would be a musician sound-checking in the chapel, as it was to be part of the service. So, there I was placing my service sheets carefully and a lady was tuning her guitar. The moment she began to sing, I froze. I turned to see her and then the penny dropped as to who she was - Alison Moyet, formally of Yazoo, and one of my favourite singers of all time. The reason I hadn't recognised her is that she had lost so much weight as to be almost unrecognisable, and to be fair, I hadn't gone into the chapel thinking who is this lady? I was totally gob-smacked. For a few short moments, I had the massive pleasure of being the only person in her audience and it was surreal. Professionalism prevailed and I resisted any ideas of doing anything other than my job. I couldn't wait to tell my brother Booger that evening about what had just happened as I know that he is a big fan as well. Wow, what a day!

Shifting emphasis back to scaring people again, Gerald was one of our staff who worked in the coffin factory. Once a week or so, we would take delivery of stock and stores that were necessary to keep our operation moving. Gerald was an old-fashioned no-nonsense individual who did everything by the book. He was like a stereotypical union leader from the 1950s. We were at the end of emptying a lorry into the workshop where the stock is moved up a floor by use of a stores lift. The stores' lift is just that; a steel cage to move stores between levels. I had this great idea to travel with the last load inside the lift in order to surprise Gerald. I know only too well that the lift is not for personnel, but making sure I had nothing sticking out from the cage, I did it anyway. As I arrived at the top level, Gerald opened the lift door and reached in as I burst out, nearly frightening him to death. I have never seen him move so fast from that day to this. He constantly reminds me that he nearly had a heart attack that day!

Occasionally, at a funeral, there will be a family request for specific vehicles to follow the family cortege. On one particular day, we were met at the home of the deceased by about a hundred motorcycles and riders, as the gentleman had belonged to a local biking club. I was driving the hearse with two family limousines in tow. Before we left the home address, one of the bikers came over to me and told me that motorbikes would act as outriders and would go ahead of us stopping any traffic so that we had a free run through the city. The journey began with us moving through a small dual carriageway on our way towards the city centre. With military-type timing, pairs of bikes would pass us and seal off any joining traffic. The route we were taking involved going onto a fast dual carriageway, but again, as we progressed, bikes were flying past us to ensure we travelled without hindrance. It was like one of those rolling traffic jams that the police use to open up a section of motorway after an accident. Once we arrived at the crematorium and began the slow ride down to the chapel, the peaceful spring morning silence was broken, by a hundred bikes or so revving and revving.

From my personal point of view, this was bettered as a spectacle later in the year when we carried out the funeral of a classic car enthusiast. Whilst they weren't acting as outriders, they made a fantastic sight. Throughout our journey through the city, about fifty classic cars followed us and looked spectacular. Everyone was stopping what they were doing to watch this lovely sight, but I think that I might have saved the best until last. By far the most memorable cortege actually brought the city to a stop. We were conducting the funeral of a lady who had been the matriarch of an ice-cream business. Behind the hearse and three limousines followed about twenty-five ice-cream vans. Everything was peaceful and solemn until we entered the grounds of the crematorium when they all started playing their ice cream van tunes. It was like Disneyland on Prozac!

When we conducted a church service, followed by a burial, there were certain activities or checks that we had to carry out as a matter of course. Some of these checks were done at the graveside. Whilst the service was going on inside the church, we would go to the grave and check things like, was the correct webbing for lowering there, were the boards placed correctly and were they safe to walk on, was the grave marker present, were the mats laid out appropriately, was there a dirt container for the blessing, etcetera?

Well, on this particular occasion, one of my colleagues, called Terry, went ahead and conducted these checks himself. Now, Terry is a lovely person with a fantastic work ethic. He is ex-army and as such, with me being ex-navy, there is always an exchange of banter. So, it broke my heart to find out that whilst he was up checking the grave, he had fallen in. He had landed on his back in his best suit and was laying six feet down in the mud. He wasn't injured but had had the wind knocked out of him. After collecting his thoughts, he realised that no one else was around and that the next people up to the grave would be the bereaved family. It probably wouldn't look too good with him climbing out of the grave just before a committal and with family looking on. After much effort and gratitude that the grave was relatively shallow, Terry emerged looking like a mud monster. To his credit, he removed his coat and cleaned himself up sufficiently with the cleaning gear that we carried on the hearses. With a few short moments to spare, we were summoned into the church to transport the coffin to the graveside. The graveside committal went fine but we were all stifling smiles at what had just happened. Poor old Terry.

My working 'dash' should have continued for at least another ten years or so, but circumstances can change very quickly. Unexpectedly, my personal situation dictated that there would be a major change of direction that was completely outside of my control.

CHAPTER 13
A DECLINE IN MENTAL HEALTH

This chapter has been by far the most difficult for me to write. When I set about writing this book, I had no fixed idea where it would end up. Having thought long and very hard about this, I feel almost a sense of moral responsibility to go ahead with things in this form, as changing circumstances have dictated where my 'working dash' goes next. On one or two occasions throughout the book, I have alluded to mental health support, or the absence of it. As you may possibly by now have realised, I have an ongoing mental health issue. My 'working dash' was cut short last year when, between my company and Occupational Health, it was decided that I was no longer fit to be in the workplace.

I think now is the time to paint a little background before we continue. My earliest knowledge of anything not being quite right goes back to 2001 when my father was diagnosed with terminal cancer. I was placed on a stress management course by the navy but the course failed to identify anything other than that I was drinking too much caffeine. As we hit 2002, my dad passed away. Being of Jewish ancestry, although not religious, a lot was expected of me, particularly as I was the eldest son. On the eve of my dad's passing, I listened to what he had to say as he lay on his death bed and I gave him permission to die. How crazy does that sound? His funeral came and passed and I spoke on behalf of the family; everything went extremely well. As the year progressed, I struggled, not only with the loss of my dad, but my marriage was failing miserably. I was re-referred onto another stress management course by the navy, but we were just going through the motions, again!

The next two years would prove to be instrumental in my fight with mental health issues. In March of 2003, I had a psychiatric review which, among other things, recommended I stay in my port area, so that I could deal with the breakup of my marriage and secure the future for my daughter. Ignoring everything that had been recommended, I was drafted to Scotland and away from my family. Whilst at my next appointment, one of my colleagues noticed a marked change in my behaviour, so much so that he reported his concerns to our second in command. The outcome of this was that I was drafted back to England, although not my base port, later in the year. During the middle part of 2003, I was diagnosed with suspected epilepsy, and, at the end of the year, divorce papers were raised. I was finally drafted back to my base port at the end of 2003 to help me deal with everything that was going on.

The year 2004 began with marriage mediation and trying to decide the best way ahead, particularly considering my daughter. Early in January, epilepsy was confirmed and I was put on medication. With this diagnosis, I had to surrender my driving licence, which took away the one pleasure I had left, driving. I moved out of the marital home in June and effectively became homeless. This was very short-lived as a very good friend of mine put me up in his home for the next year or so. I was very uncomfortable with the epilepsy diagnosis and requested a second opinion. I had done this for two reasons. Firstly, the doctor who diagnosed me was a trainee and he kept popping next door to see the specialist, who, for the record, never consulted me once. Secondly, there seemed this preoccupation with my 'grand mal', which had happened 25 years earlier. In October of 2004, just as my 'decree absolute' came through, I got my second opinion in Birmingham and was told unequivocally that I didn't have epilepsy. Much later on, I found out that these 'fits', as I was calling them, were, in actual fact, panic attacks, and that was what I had unknowingly been suffering with. With my driving licence now on its way back to me, I was at least able to be mobile again, although this process took five months. As we moved into 2005, the year started with me going to court to settle finances with my now ex-wife.

I also managed to scrape enough together for a deposit on a home of my own. This was very important to me as I wanted somewhere where my daughter would feel safe and comfortable visiting.

I left the navy in 2007, and, after a short spell on the cruise liners, I decided that I wanted to be closer to my daughter and new wife-to-be. Surprisingly, certainly to me, my mental health continued on a slow downhill spiral. I was becoming far less tolerant and much more easily agitated. I was becoming moody and angered more easily. I put a lot of this down to resettlement in civvy street and de-militarising, and tried to work through it. In 2013, I sought permission from my bosses to attend a mental health support package. After a brief period with one carer, he passed me on to more specialised counselling. I took a few things from my counsellor and continued with life. In 2016, whilst at a family party, I was attacked from behind by my daughter, who was extremely drunk. I pulled her off my back and just held her on the floor where she could no longer attack me. Everybody witnessed this unprovoked attack except my first wife, who had been in the toilet. When she arrived, all she could see was me holding our daughter on the floor and me covered in blood, my blood! She elected to attack me as well, and right in front of my mother, my daughter's grandmother! After numerous attempts at reconciliation with my daughter, we haven't spoken from that day to this, but I do miss her.

Midway through 2018, we had a major reshuffle planned for the workplace, with threats of redundancies and shifting to new roles. This process caused much concern, worry, and stress. As we progressed through the year, there was a lot of uncertainty and so planning was difficult, to say the least. The goalposts were moved several times during the run-up to the changes. Personally, I had a particularly difficult period. I have a well-documented back injury, and with it go certain physical limitations, which are, and always have been, known by my bosses. I was told that I couldn't take redundancy and that I would have to take on a different role. The issue was that I was physically unable to do the new job. I was told at this point that there was no redundancy and no other options for me. This frustrated me over a protracted period of time as I couldn't understand why I was being re-tasked to an area that I couldn't physically work. Over the next few weeks and months, I slipped into depression. I had little or no motivation to do anything and suffered some other side effects such as erratic or no sleep, no libido, lethargy, extremely bad nightmares, and panic attacks.

I was by now off sick, on psychotropic medication, and at home. I could not face leaving the house, and when my counsellor asked me to explain how I felt, I explained, "Imagine you are a kid and you are in a tent, a little 2-man tent, in a field, on a lovely summer's day. There is grass and a brook running nearby; there are butterflies, and birds singing. You go to step out from your tent but suddenly, a fear of the unknown overcomes you. You can't explain it but it will not allow you out, so you zip up the tent and stay within the sanctuary of the tent." I was by now having panic attacks fairly regularly but at least I was recognising them for what they were; in the early days, I thought it was a massive heart attack. Indeed, I almost cut short an American road trip because I had no understanding of what was going on.

My regional manager at work recognised my state of mind and offered to come to my home for a once-a-month meeting, which I agreed to. This was on condition that my wife could be there as I was forgetting an awful lot. It was only on about her third visit that we discussed in any depth the future options. What came out of our conversation absolutely astounded me, but explained some of the crazy decisions. Human Resources had absolutely no record of my back injury. As far as they were concerned, I was as fit as a fiddle. When confronted with this information, I dug out historical paperwork which supported my saying that the company was aware of my back condition and had recorded it accordingly. I even showed her that on two separate occasions, I had hurt my back in minor lifting incidences, and, on the accident forms, I had referred to my accident as not being the cause of my back injury. It now made sense why they didn't offer me redundancy and were placing me in an unattainable role. My regional manager confronted HR about this but it would seem that my line manager and his boss, the hub manager, had never acted on my paperwork and as both had moved on, there was no punitive action that could be taken. Thankfully, I have always been meticulous with my paperwork and could back up what I was saying. After an absence of about five months, I returned to work where my regional manager had made some comprehensive changes to accommodate my mental health requirements. She had actually been instrumental in whether I returned at all.

It was about this time that I started working with our local mental health support group again. I attended Cognitive Behavioural Therapy, or CBT, but found that I was just going through the motions rather than actually moving towards a place of positive mental health. I had a few classroom sessions but found them to be of no help; in fact, they were bringing on my anxiety. I actually had a panic attack during the lesson. After classes, I was passed to a counsellor for a number of sessions and to be evaluated. After a period of some months, I was referred to a higher level of more in-depth counselling. These sessions went on for some twenty weeks and I built up a good rapport with Kathy, my counsellor. At the end of these sessions, I felt that we had made good progress but didn't feel that we had solved any issues. Kathy asked me how I felt about going about things on my own when the sessions finished. I told her that it was like I was a bird in a big hand where I felt safe, but now

I was going to be released into the world and I wasn't sure I was ready. Having now exhausted all avenues that I believed were open to me, I decided to try to reclaim responsibility for my life. It was the run-up to Christmas, so, unusually, I indulged myself in that. Christmas came and went, and, after one or two issues with changes in my psychotropic medication, I settled down to dealing with everyday life. Then Wham! The pandemic hit.

As an undertaker, you would be the last person who could work from home. We were seeing unprecedented numbers of deaths and our workload increased dramatically as the pandemic got a grip. There was much more anger at funerals, predominantly from families of deceased who had died in nursing or care homes. They were, of course, unable to say their goodbyes in person and many were quite verbal about it. Uncertainties about travelling in limousines and attendance at funeral services continued to change as government guidelines altered. Just prior to the pandemic hitting, I had spoken to my family doctor about the prospect of reducing my psychotropic drug intake. His response was to wait for maybe six months until everything was settled and then we could look at it. I'm still waiting for things to settle! During the pandemic, it was as if time itself stood still. We were being separated and isolated within our working environment, only really coming together to carry a coffin. Kathy, my counsellor, was a long and distant memory, but I believed that I had exhausted all avenues of support. I also believed that there were more important issues going on than my own mental health. As a result, I went for about eighteen months without any support when, in actual fact, I should have sought more help. I felt that Kathy had given me the tools to cope and that eventually, these methods would kick in, which, of course, never happened. Additionally, and I make no apology for this, I felt that I had burdened the mental health support team once and so to do it again would be selfish.

In early 2021, and for no apparent reason, my new line manager decided to put me back on fleet-manning again, which is what I had been doing before the changes instigated by my regional manager. Both she and my line manager believed that this would be in my best interest now and in the longer term. I accepted what they said and continued in the new/old role. Some issues began to raise themselves again, the most obvious being that the directors didn't really know the circumstances of my employ and they were unaware of my limitations. I am quite happy to speak up for myself but I am not about to discuss personal and confidential issues with every Tom, Dick and Harry. As a result of this non-communication from my bosses, there was to be a row between my hub manager and myself. I exploded with rage at what he had said and the insensitivity with which he had said it. Accusations were made by me about mismanagement and the air turned blue for a few short moments. This angered me no end and I left the workplace straight away in order to remove myself from a volatile situation. Having spoken to my doctor, I took time off sick as this row had set me back no end.

This time being away from the workplace was totally different from the last time. After initially trying to discipline me for my part in the row, the case was dropped as the six witnesses supported my story and stated that I had done no wrong. The monthly meetings were passed down to the line manager this time, who, for the record, was in his first three months in his first admin job. I am not blaming him; he did a thorough and professional job, but the management support had dropped two levels. Unlike before, the monthly meetings were conducted over the telephone from my home. My mental state was probably now worse than ever. I was shutting myself off from everyone, including friends and family. I wouldn't leave the house for anything, I had absolutely no motivation and was in a very low mood. Times were dark!

Moving forward a few weeks and I was contacted by a Department of Works and Pensions or DWP-appointed counsellor whose name was Jane. It had been explained to me that I would need psychotherapy by my local mental health support group, but that the waiting list was about forty weeks. In the meantime, Jane would act as my safety officer and support me as best she could. This arrangement would only stay in place as long as

I remained employed. Jane and I worked together for about five months, developing a sense of trust and almost friendship, and her help and guidance was my main source of inspiration. Our weekly telephone calls were my main connection with the outside world and the one thing I looked forward to. Jane became more than just my safety officer or advisor; she became my beacon of light in a darkened world. As 2021 progressed, between my company and Occupational Health, they decided that I would be unfit to return to the workplace for the foreseeable future and so they sought a medical discharge. This couldn't have come at a worse time, as I now felt more vulnerable than ever. Jane supported me through the darkest of times. On two separate occasions, I seriously considered suicide, and when I say I was seriously considering it, this was no cry for help. I planned how to kill myself and what I would need to do it. I also chose the venue and how to time my suicide in order to minimise the chances of my wife finding me. These thoughts were totally alien to me; it was something I had never contemplated at any stage of my life before. The big question was, what caused my thought process to go down this avenue?

The easy answer is I don't really know. My mood was extremely low, I had absolutely no motivation and my depression was as bad as ever. Since the onset of my mental health issues, I have developed a habit of catastrophising and ruminating. What this means in layman's terms is that I think only the worse of any situation and I ponder or think about everything in far too much detail. All of these things seemed to come to a head at the same time making it very difficult for me to behave rationally. Thankfully, on both occasions, these thoughts passed fairly quickly and I began to function again. It is about a year since the last of these episodes and I really do hope that there is no repeat.

In due course, I was medically discharged from the workplace with no real idea as to what to do next. Because of my catastrophising, I plummeted into a downhill spiral. What will I do, how can I find work, how will I pay the bills, who would employ a 64-year-old with a back injury and a serious mental health problem? The singularly biggest issue I had to deal with was that Jane was no longer allowed to work with me as I was no longer employed. This was a real slap in the face to me. I was down, things weren't good, and the one good thing in my life, other than my wife, was my relationship with my safety officer, Jane. It was as if the safety net was taken away and I was left very much alone. It would be about five very long months before I would receive any mental health support at all.

I have noticed, surprisingly, in recent months, that my personality and character seem to have gone through some sort of transition. I feel much more relaxed about things in general. I feel that I am much more easy-going, I feel less angry, less judgmental and more empathetic than I have ever been. I understand the chemical effects of psychotropic drugs and accept that they play their part, yet, I also accept that I may be on medication for quite some time yet.

Recently, a space was found for me with a psychotherapist whose name is Danielle. Because of the pandemic, we only speak on the telephone, but this suits me as I still have trouble going outdoors or mixing with people. We have already built up a rapport and are trying to pick up where Jane and I left off some months back.

Given my belief that my character might be somewhat changed, I tried a little experiment; I asked Dale, who was my on-call partner for quite some years and is a very close friend, and my wife, to choose between me as I used to be, and me as I am now. I wanted to know which of the two was more preferable and these two people know me better than anyone. Both knew me before my mental health issues when I was less tolerant, moodier, less empathetic, more aggressive, (not in a violent way), and more of an 'alpha male'! This was also when I was much more sociable. To my surprise, they both prefer me as I am today but without the issues I am dealing with. The reason I wanted to try this 'experiment' was, as I alluded to in chapter 4, according to my parents, I underwent a major character change after my 'grand mal' back in the 1970s. As best my memory serves, and listening to my parents, the changes back then mirror the changes now. Over the many years since my 'grand mal', my parents have always said that they preferred the old me. As a result of this exercise, I have a burning question inside - is it possible for the medication and counselling that I am on to be taking my brain back to where it originally was prior to the 'grand mal'? I await the answer to that question in earnest.

I want to talk about some of the physical effects that this journey has taken me on, which, in themselves, complicate my recuperation. When I left the Royal Navy, which, on the face of it, was somewhere near the beginning of this journey, I weighed around 106 kilos or 16.5 stone in old money. I now weigh 136.5 kilos or 21 stone 5lbs. Even allowing for a complete change in lifestyle and diet, this is excessive. Most of this weight has been gained in the last year, which, coincidentally, is when my mental health has been at its worse. Diabetes is staring me in the face; indeed, I am being monitored closely at this time. Because my psychotropic medication has a constipating effect, I have to take laxatives twice a day and have had to do so for the last two and a half years. I have absolutely no pattern to my sleep. I can sleep for twelve hours uninterrupted, get up, and then be tired an hour later. I can sleep during the daytime which is something I never did before. Equally, I can go to bed and lie awake most of the night because my active thoughts won't allow me to sleep. My libido has nosedived, which isn't easy to accept, but it is what it is. I am very lethargic and seem to have no energy, which

I believe relates to low motivation. I quite often have to remind myself that I am not lazy, far from it, and my wife continually reminds me of this. I have suffered with mild eczema since I was a young adult but my skin condition has flared up to uncomfortable levels in the last few years. Whilst I know that stress aggravates my condition, it is medication that controls it.

To try and make light of the situation, I have recently added two tattoos to my body art. I now have a large phoenix carrying a scroll saying "post tenebras lux" on my left forearm. The phoenix is to signify the re-birth or new life coming from the ashes of despair and the Latin says "after darkness comes light" which was my second ship's motto, and, I thought, very appropriate. In chapter 7, I explained how, in a day of drunkenness on the beach, I started proceedings that would ultimately leave my left arm with three scars on it. As part of my recuperation, I also had a tattoo to cover these scars. The tattoo is a partially opened zipper with a monster's hand beginning to emerge from inside me. This tattoo reminds me of the journey that I have been on to date, and that the monster is still potentially in there.

After what has felt like considerable progress over the past few months, an initial diagnosis was made as to what my mental health issue might actually be. Labelling my condition was important to me because it reassured me that I really did have an ongoing condition. I have Complex Post Traumatic Stress Disorder, or CPTSD, and General Anxiety Disorder. I also have Panic Disorder which quite often goes alongside CPTSD. The panic disorder, which is usually prevalent in women, would go some way to explaining my agora-phobia and my reluctance to mix with people. Progress with my psychotherapist is steady but slow. There are no quick fixes in this area but I am reassured by our new-found relationship. One thing I really must learn is not to expect too much of myself too soon. I have recently had minor setbacks with panic attacks because I believe I was trying to bite off more than I could chew. Having agreed a way ahead with Danielle, we are aiming for the medium and longer-term, rather than just for now.

Since I began venturing again into the great out-doors, I have, with much trepidation, started a weekly pilgrimage to a local restaurant which I shall call the breakfast club. This visit serves two purposes; initially, it gets me out of the house and into town where I can try to deal with my panic disorder. I have to make my way through a busy town centre in order to get to the restaurant. Secondly, and as a reward for taking on a visit to town, I get a lovely Mexican breakfast in a peaceful atmosphere where the staff are fantastic and the food is superb. Since I have been visiting the breakfast club, I have struck up a relationship with Tom, who used to be the general manager. Tom is aware of my journey through mental health illness and is extremely empa-thetic. Tom has also made me even more aware of just how widespread mental health issues are, particularly in the workplace.

Whenever I visit the breakfast club, I go through the full gamut of emotions and feelings. Before I leave home, I have to build up the courage to go outside. I drive to the car park, which is something I've only just got back to being able to do; I do this during the morning when it is quieter on the roads and park in the corner of the car park. During my journey thus far, I may well feel the initial onset of a panic attack, in that my heart begins racing, I get palpitations and my temperature rises. I have to re-build up the courage to leave the car and walk through town to the breakfast club. During this walk, my senses are very sharp and I am constantly looking for quieter areas to walk in. My panic attack symptoms have receded a little and I am fully focused on getting to the club. On my arrival, I am quite hot and my heart is still racing. Once I get upstairs and into the sanctuary of the club, I begin to settle. I always sit in the far corner - the staff afford me this privilege - and I settle down listening to the background music. Almost immediately after I arrive, a jug of cold fresh water arrives at my table, which is extremely welcome.

The breakfast club is like an old-fashioned gentleman's club, with quality fittings and old portraits and pictures adorning the walls. The staff are very well turned out and very attentive to your needs. They also, and to me very importantly, seem to have the time to talk to you or just to listen to you. This social interaction I have found invaluable on my road to repair. After a beautiful breakfast, I find myself fully relaxed and contented, and ready to face the journey back to the car. My return journey is never as anxiety-filled as the journey out, but I am extremely happy when I arrive back at my car. On my arrival back at home, I feel I am back in my safe place and I am quite proud of what I have just achieved.

CHAPTER 14
IN RETIREMENT

My 'working dash' was severely curtailed last year, 2021, when my mental illness became too much for my company to accommodate. Having now slipped relatively seamlessly into retirement, I find that I have time on my hands, which is something I seldom had whilst I was working. During the last few months, I have thought long and hard about my life so far, and the choices I have made. I have no regrets about the avenues and opportunities that were presented to me. I spent thirty-five years with the Royal Navy travelling to some of the most beautiful places imaginable.

I have spent time in South Georgia and Antarctica watching baby penguins grow and have also been in awe of the southern ice packs. I have spent time on Copacabana Beach and viewed Rio de Janeiro from the top of Sugarloaf Mountain. I was once stranded in the Grand Canyon when our helicopter broke down (what rotten luck) and I have driven a Ford Mustang convertible on route 66 and along America's West Coast. I viewed polar bears in the Arctic Circle and elephants in South Africa, as well as visiting Cape Canaveral to watch a rocket launch. There have been times spent on some of the most beautiful beaches that the Caribbean has to offer and visits to over a hundred countries so far, sampling cuisines from all over the world, and I have embraced cultures from East and West. For my involvement in operational campaigns, I have been very well decorated. Yes, there were difficult times and some difficult decisions along the way, but I have no regrets.

I didn't feel that I could write a book about my 'working dash' without referencing the beautiful & tranquil South Georgia.

Here is the author getting up close and personal with elephant seals, king penguins and their chicks.

Young elephant seals at the ruins of an old whaling station

After clinically dying in the 1970s and undergoing certain changes, I re-evaluated things and got on as best I could. My first marriage failed but from it came my beautiful daughter. Without the experience of my first marriage, I probably would never have met my current wife, so I am trying to look at things as a stepping stone to where I want to be. I am trying, very hard, just to be able to re-join society as an ordinary functioning person. I want to be able to freely roam where I wish without the fears that this brings. I need to re-learn my communication skills and practise them. I would love to be more confident again and maybe even occasionally laugh at things. I accepted that I was broken, so I, with help, am effecting repairs and, in the fullness of time, will put all of this behind me.

Having left the Royal Navy and after a short period on the cruise liners, I became an undertaker.

I approached this business in much the same way as I had the navy. I learned new experiences, forged new friendships, and found out a lot more about my compassionate side. Whilst I was in the navy and during my time as an undertaker, I met quite a few famous people on my travels: I shook hands with Sid James, met Barbara Windsor, and had the honour to meet three Kings and two Queens. I have exchanged views with football pundit and ex-soccer star Charlie Nicholas and even told Keith Chegwin that he looks much better with his clothes on! On one particular occasion, I was chatting up a young lady in Dubai who was lounging in the sun. She was totally adorned with gold jewellery, probably more than H. Samuel's. After about an hour, her husband turned up and was none other than the larger-than-life football manager, Malcolm Allison.

In other words, for someone who is dealing with mental health issues, I have previously, and continue to have, a very positive outlook, as there is still a lot of living to be done. Fortunately, I have overcome most obstacles that have been placed before me and I have moved on to the next phase in my life. I am dealing with my mental health issues and the limitations that it brings as best I am able. My psychotherapist is a massive help and between us, we are making good progress. Accepting that I needed help in the first place was probably the biggest hurdle to date. Accepting the need for medication was another.

Whilst my 'working dash' is possibly fin-ished, my 'life's dash' certainly isn't.

N.B. At this particular time in my recovery, there are atrocities being carried out in Ukraine. My journey back to mental health fitness is being curtailed by my cata-strophising over the potential outcome of this tragic set of events. Seeing bodies and body bags takes me back to being an undertaker and reminds me that life is so valuable; it also reminds me of my own mortality. As an ex-serviceman, I know that I live within a mile of one of three strategic targets. A dictatorship without account-ability is a dangerous thing. I hope things settle quickly and the world can breathe safely once again.

Dear reader,

If you have enjoyed this book could I please ask you to leave a review on Amazon or Goodreads or any social media platform that you are involved with?

Many Thanks, Martin

ACKNOWLEDGMENTS

Firstly, I would like to thank my brother 'Booger' for his patience and for always being there when I needed to bounce ideas off him. He also gave me solid advice when I was at a crossroads and when I needed it most.

Secondly, I would like to personally thank Dave Cheeseman, a true friend and someone who was always there.

Thirdly, I would like to thank all of the mental health support services that have been invaluable to me in very difficult times. I would particularly like to thank Jean Langford for her support and encouragement.

Fourthly, I would like to thank Scott from Publishing Push, for helping me navigate through the difficult process of getting the book ready for print.

Finally, and most importantly, I would like to thank my long-suffering wife Sarah, without whose support, encouragement and understanding this book would never have been completed.

Printed in Great Britain
by Amazon

42316753R00126